DATE DUE			

SHAKESPEARE AND THE MODERN STAGE

AMS PRESS

NEW YORK

SHAKESPEARE AND THE MODERN STAGE

WITH OTHER ESSAYS

BY SIDNEY LEE

AUTHOR OF "GREAT ENGLISHMEN OF THE SIXTEENTH CENTURY,"
"A LIFE OF WILLIAM SHAKESPEARE," ETC.

NEW YORK
CHARLES SCRIBNER'S SONS
1906

Library of Congress Cataloging in Publication Data

Lee, Sir Sidney, 1859-1926.
  Shakespeare and the modern stage.

    1. Shakespeare, William, 1564-1616—Addresses,
essays, lectures. I. Title.
PR2890.L37   1974   822.3'3   74-172042
ISBN 0-404-03929-4

Reprinted from the edition of 1906, New York
First AMS edition published in 1974
Manufactured in the United States of America

AMS PRESS INC.
NEW YORK, N.Y. 10003

PREFACE

THE eleven papers which are collected here were
written between 1899 and 1905. With the exception of one, entitled "Aspects of Shakespeare's Philosophy," which is now printed for the first time,
all were published in periodicals in the course of
those six years. The articles treat of varied aspects
of Shakespearean drama, its influences and traditions, but I think that all may be credited with
sufficient unity of intention to warrant their com-
bination in a single volume. Their main endeavour
is to survey Shakespearean drama in relation to
modern life, and to illustrate its living force in
current affairs. Even in the papers which embody
researches in sixteenth- or seventeenth-century dramatic history, I have sought to keep in view the
bearings of the past on the present. A large portion
of the book discusses, as its title indicates, methods
of representing Shakespeare on the modern stage.
The attempt is there made to define, in the light of
experience, the conditions which are best calculated
to conserve or increase Shakespeare's genuine vitality
in the theatre of our own day.

In revising the work for the press, I have deemed
it advisable to submit the papers to a somewhat
rigorous verbal revision. Errors have been corrected,

chronological ambiguities due to lapse of time have
been removed, passages have been excised in order
to avoid repetition, and reference to ephemeral
events which deserve no permanent chronicle have
been omitted. But, substantially, the articles retain
the shape in which they were originally penned.
The point of view has undergone no modification.
In the essays dealing with the theatres of our own
time, I have purposely refrained from expanding or
altering argument or illustration by citing Shakespearean performances or other theatrical enterprises which have come to birth since the papers were
first written. In the last year or two there have
been several Shakespearean revivals of notable interest, and some new histrionic triumphs have been
won. Within the same period, too, at least half a
dozen new plays of serious literary aim have gained
the approval of contemporary critics. These features
of current dramatic history are welcome to playgoers of literary tastes; but I have attempted no
survey of them, because signs are lacking that any
essential change has been wrought by them in the
general theatrical situation. My aim is to deal with
dominant principles which underlie the past and
present situation, rather than with particular episodes
or personalities, the real value of which the future
has yet to determine.

My best thanks are due to my friend Sir James
Knowles, the proprietor and editor of *The Nineteenth
Century and After*, for permission to reproduce the
four articles, entitled respectively, "Shakespeare and
the Modern Stage," "Shakespeare in Oral Tradition,"
"Shakespeare in France," and "The Commemoration of Shakespeare in London." To Messrs Smith,

Elder & Co., I am indebted for permission to print here the articles on "Mr Benson and Shakespearean Drama," and "Shakespeare and Patriotism," both of which originally appeared in *The Cornhill Magazine*. The paper on "Pepys and Shakespeare" was first printed in the *Fortnightly Review;* that on "Shakespeare and the Elizabethan Playgoer" in "An English Miscellany, presented to Dr Furnivall in honour of his seventy-fifth birthday" (1901); that on "The Municipal Theatre" in the *New Liberal Review;* and that on "A Peril of Shakespearean Research" in *The Author*. The proprietors of these publications have courteously given me permission to include the articles in this volume. The essay on "Aspects of Shakespeare's Philosophy" was prepared for the purposes of a popular lecture, and has not been in type before.

In a note at the foot of the opening page of each essay, I mention the date when it was originally published. An analytical list of contents and an index will, I hope, increase any utility which may attach to the volume.

SIDNEY LEE.

1st October, 1906.

CONTENTS

CONTENTS

V

Mr Benson and Shakespearean Drama

VI

The Municipal Theatre

VII

Aspects of Shakespeare's Philosophy

X

SHAKESPEARE IN FRANCE

XI

THE COMMEMORATION OF SHAKESPEARE IN LONDON

SHAKESPEARE AND THE MODERN STAGE

I

SHAKESPEARE AND THE MODERN STAGE[1]

I

WITHOUT "the living comment and interpretation of the theatre," Shakespeare's work is, for the rank and file of mankind, "a deep well without a wheel or a windlass." It is true that the whole of the spiritual treasures which Shakespeare's dramas hoard will never be disclosed to the mere playgoer, but "a large, a very large, proportion of that indefinite all" may be revealed to him on the stage, and, if he be no patient reader, will be revealed to him nowhere else.

There are earnest students of Shakespeare who scorn the theatre and arrogate to themselves in the library, often with some justification, a greater capacity for apprehending and appreciating Shakespeare than is at the command of the ordinary playgoer or actor. But let Sir Oracle of the study, however full and deep be his knowledge, "use all gently." Let him bear in mind that his vision also has its limitations, and that student, actor, and spectator

[1] This paper was first printed in *The Nineteenth Century*, January, 1900.

of Shakespeare's plays are all alike exploring a measureless region of philosophy and poetry, "round which no comprehension has yet drawn the line of circumspection, so as to say to itself 'I have seen the whole.'" Actor and student may look at Shakespeare's text from different points of view; but there is always as reasonable a chance that the efficient actor may disclose the full significance of some speech or scene which escapes the efficient student, as that the student may supply the actor's lack of insight.

It is, indeed, comparatively easy for a student of literature to support the proposition that Shakespeare can be, and ought to be, represented on the stage. But it is difficult to define the ways and means of securing practical observance of the precept. For some years there has been a widening divergence of view respecting methods of Shakespearean production. Those who defend in theory the adaptability of Shakespeare to the stage are at variance with the leading managers, who alone possess the power of conferring on the Shakespearean drama theatrical interpretation. In the most influential circles of the theatrical profession it has become a commonplace to assert that Shakespearean drama cannot be successfully produced, cannot be rendered tolerable to any substantial section of the playgoing public, without a plethora of scenic spectacle and gorgeous costume, much of which the student regards as superfluous and inappropriate. An accepted tradition of the modern stage ordains that every revival of a Shakespearean play at a leading theatre shall base some part of its claim to public favour on its spectacular magnificence.

The dramatic interest of Shakespearean drama is, in fact, deemed by the manager to be inadequate to satisfy the necessary commercial purposes of the theatre. The average purveyor of public entertainment reckons Shakespeare's plays among tasteless and colourless commodities, which only become marketable when they are reinforced by the independent arts of music and painting. Shakespeare's words must be spoken to musical accompaniments specially prepared for the occasion. Pictorial tableaux, even though they suggest topics without relevance to the development of the plot, have at times to be interpolated in order to keep the attention of the audience sufficiently alive.

One deduction to be drawn from this position of affairs is irrefutable. Spectacular embellishments are so costly that, according to the system now in vogue, the performance of a play of Shakespeare involves heavy financial risks. It is equally plain that, unless the views of theatrical managers undergo revolution, these risks are likely to become greater rather than smaller. The natural result is that in London, the city which sets the example to most English-speaking communities, Shakespearean revivals are comparatively rare; they take place at uncertain intervals, and only those plays are viewed with favour by the London manager which lend themselves in his opinion to more or less ostentatious spectacle, and to the interpolation of music and dancing.

It is ungrateful to criticise adversely any work the production of which entails the expenditure of much thought and money. More especially is it distasteful when the immediate outcome is, as in the

case of many Shakespearean revivals at the great
West-end theatres of London, the giving of pleasure
to large sections of the community. That is in itself
a worthy object. But it is open to doubt whether,
from the sensible literary point of view, the managerial activity be well conceived or to the public
advantage. It is hard to ignore a fundamental
flaw in the manager's central position. The pleasure
which recent Shakespearean revivals offer the spectator reaches him mainly through the eye. That
is the manager's avowed intention. Yet no one
would seriously deny that the Shakespearean drama
appeals, both primarily and ultimately, to the head
and to the heart. Whoever seeks, therefore, by
the production of Shakespearean drama chiefly to
please the spectator's eye shows scant respect both
for the dramatist and for the spectator, however
unwittingly he tends to misrepresent the one and
to mislead the other in a particular of first-rate
importance. Indeed, excess in scenic display does
worse than restrict opportunities of witnessing
Shakespeare's plays on the stage in London and
other large cities of England and America. It is
to be feared that such excess either weakens or dis-
torts the just and proper influence of Shakespeare's
work. If these imputations can be sustained, then
it follows that the increased and increasing expense
which is involved in the production of Shakespeare's
plays ought on grounds of public policy to be
diminished.

II

Every stage representation of a play requires
sufficient scenery and costume to produce in the

audience that illusion of environment which the text invites. Without so much scenery or costume the words fail to get home to the audience. In comedies dealing with concrete conditions of modern society, the stage presentation necessarily relies to a very large extent for its success on the realism of the scenic appliances. In plays which, dealing with the universal and less familiar conditions of life, appeal to the highest faculties of thought and imagination, the pursuit of realism in the scenery tends to destroy the full significance of the illusion which it ought to enforce. In the case of plays straightforwardly treating of contemporary affairs, the environment which it is sought to reproduce is familiar and easy of imitation. In the case of drama, which involves larger spheres of fancy and feeling, the environment is unfamiliar and admits of no realistic imitation. The wall-paper and furniture of Mrs. So-and-so's drawing-room in Belgravia or Derbyshire can be transferred bodily to the stage. Prospero's deserted island does not admit of the like translation.

Effective suggestion of the scene of *The Tempest* is all that can be reasonably attempted or desired. Plays which are wrought of purest imaginative texture call solely for a scenic setting which should convey effective suggestion. The machinery to be employed for the purpose of effective suggestion should be simple and unobtrusive. If it be complex and obtrusive, it defeats "the purpose of playing" by exaggerating for the spectator the inevitable interval between the visionary and indeterminate limits of the scene which the poet imagines and the cramped and narrow bounds which the stage renders practicable. That perilous interval can only be ef-

fectually bridged by scenic art, which is applied
with an apt judgment and a light hand. Anything
that aims at doing more than satisfy the condition
essential to the effective suggestion of the scenic
environment of Shakespearean drama is, from the
literary and logical points of view, "wasteful and
ridiculous excess." [1]

But it is not only a simplification of scenic appliances that is needed. Other external incidents
of production require revision. Spectacular methods
of production entail the employment of armies of
silent supernumeraries to whom are allotted functions wholly ornamental and mostly impertinent.
Here, too, reduction is desirable in the interest of
the true significance of drama. No valid reason
can be adduced why persons should appear on the
stage who are not precisely indicated by the text of
the play or by the authentic stage directions. When
Cæsar is buried, it is essential to produce in the
audience the illusion that a crowd of Roman citizens
is taking part in the ceremony. But quality comes
here before quantity. The fewer the number of
supernumeraries by whom the needful illusion is
effected, the greater the merit of the performance,
the more convincing the testimony borne to the skill
of the stage-manager. Again, no processions of
psalm-singing priests and monks contribute to the
essential illusion in the historical plays. Nor does
the text of *The Merchant of Venice* demand any

---

[1] A minor practical objection, from the dramatic point of view,
to realistic scenery is the long pause its setting on the stage often
renders inevitable between the scenes. Intervals of the kind,
which always tend to blunt the dramatic point of the play,
especially in the case of tragic masterpieces, should obviously be
as brief as possible.

assembly of Venetian townsfolk, however pic-
turesquely attired, sporting or chaffering with one
another on the Rialto, when Shylock enters to
ponder Antonio's request for a loan. An interpolated tableau is indefensible, and "though it
make the unskilful laugh, cannot but make the
judicious grieve." In *Antony and Cleopatra* the
pageant of Cleopatra's voyage up the river Cydnus
to meet her lover Antony should have no existence
outside the gorgeous description given of it by
Enobarbus.

III

What would be the practical effects of a stern
resolve on the part of theatrical managers to sim-
plify the scenic appliances and to reduce the supernumerary staff when they are producing Shakespearean drama? The replies will be in various
keys. One result of simplification is obvious. There
would be so much more money in the manager's
pocket after he had paid the expenses of production. If his outlay were smaller, the sum that he
expended in the production of one play of Shakespeare on the current over-elaborate scale would
cover the production of two or three pieces mounted
with simplicity and with a strict adherence to the
requirements of the text. In such an event, the
manager would be satisfied with a shorter run for
each play.

On the other hand, supporters of the existing
system allege that no public, which is worth the
counting, would interest itself in Shakespeare's
plays, if they were robbed of scenic upholstery and

spectacular display. This estimate rests on insecure foundations. That section of the London public, which is genuinely interested in Shakespearean drama for its own sake, is prone to distrust the modern theatrical manager, and as things are, for the most part avoids the theatre altogether. The student stays at home to read Shakespeare at his fire-side.

It may be admitted that the public to which Shakespeare in his purity makes appeal is not very large. It is clearly not large enough to command continuous runs of plays for months, or even weeks. But therein lies no cause for depression. Long runs of a single play of Shakespeare bring more evil than good in their train. They develop in even the most efficient acting a soulless mechanism. The literary beauty of the text is obliterated by repetition from the actors' minds. Unostentatious mounting of the Shakespearean plays, however efficient be the acting with which it is associated, may always fail to "please the million"; it may be "caviare to the general." Nevertheless, the sagacious manager, who, by virtue of comparatively inexpensive settings and in alliance with a well-chosen company of efficient actors and actresses, is able at short intervals to produce a succession of Shakespeare's plays, may reasonably expect to attract a small but steady and sufficient support from the intelligent section of London playgoers, and from the home-reading students of Shakespeare, who are not at present playgoers at all.

IV

The practical manager, who naturally seeks pecuniary profit from his ventures, insists that these suggestions are counsels of perfection and these anticipations wild and fantastic dreams. His last word is that by spectacular method Shakespeare can alone be made to "pay" in the theatre. But are we here on perfectly secure ground? Has the commercial success attending the spectacular production of Shakespeare been invariably so conspicuous as to put summarily out of court, on the purely commercial ground, the method of simplicity? The pecuniary results are public knowledge in the case of the two most strenuous and prolonged endeavours to give Shakespeare the splendours of spectacle which have yet been completed on the London stage. What is the message of these two efforts in mere pecuniary terms?

Charles Kean may be regarded as the founder of the modern spectacular system, though it had some precedents and has been developed since his day. Charles Kean, between 1851 and 1859, persistently endeavoured by prodigal and brilliant display to make the production of Shakespeare an enterprise of profit at the Princess's Theatre, London. The scheme proved pecuniarily disastrous.

Subsequently Kean's mantle was assumed by the late Sir Henry Irving, the greatest of recent actors and stage-managers, who in many regards conferred incalculable benefits on the theatre-going public and on the theatrical profession. Throughout the last quarter of the last century, Irving gave the spectacular and scenic system in the production of Shakespeare every advantage that it could

derive from munificent expenditure and the co-
operation of highly endowed artists. He could
justly claim a finer artistic sentiment and a higher
histrionic capacity than Charles Kean possessed.
Yet Irving announced not long before his death
that he lost on his Shakespearean productions a
hundred thousand pounds. Sir Henry added:

The enormous cost of a Shakespearean production on the liberal and elaborate scale which the
public is now accustomed to expect makes it almost
impossible for any manager—I don't care who it is
—to pursue a continuous policy of Shakespeare for
many years with any hope of profit in the long run.

In face of this authoritative pronouncement, it
must be conceded that the spectacular system has
been given, within recent memory, every chance of
succeeding, and, as far as recorded testimony is
available, has been, from the commercial point of
view, a failure.

Meanwhile, during and since the period when
Sir Henry Irving filled the supreme place among
producers of Shakespeare on the stage, the simple
method of Shakespearean production has been
given no serious chance. The anticipation of its
pecuniary failure has not been put in satisfactory
conditions to any practical test. The last time that
it was put to a sound practical test it did not fail.
While Irving was a boy, Phelps at Sadler's Wells
Theatre gave, in well-considered conditions, the
simple method a trial. Phelps's playhouse was situ-
ated in the unfashionable neighbourhood of Islington.
But the prophets of evil, who were no greater strangers to Phelps's generation than they are to our
own, were themselves confuted by his experience.

V

On the 27th of May, 1844, Phelps, a most intelligent actor and a serious student of Shakespeare, opened the long-disused Sadler's Wells Theatre in partnership with Mrs. Warner, a capable actress, whose rendering of Imogen went near perfection. Their design was inspired by "the hope," they wrote in an unassuming address, "of eventually rendering Sadler's Wells what a theatre ought to be, a place for justly representing the works of our great dramatic poets." This hope they went far to realise. The first play that they produced was *Macbeth*.

Phelps continued to control Sadler's Wells Theatre for more than eighteen years. During that period he produced, together with many other English plays of classical repute, no fewer than thirty-one of the thirty-seven great dramas which came from Shakespeare's pen. In his first season, besides *Macbeth* he set forth *Hamlet, King John, Henry VIII., The Merchant of Venice, Othello,* and *Richard III.* To these he added in the course of his second season *Julius Cæsar, King Lear,* and *The Winter's Tale. Henry IV.,* part I., *Measure for Measure, Romeo and Juliet,* and *The Tempest* followed in his third season; *As You Like It, Cymbeline, The Merry Wives of Windsor,* and *Twelfth Night,* in his fourth. Each succeeding season saw further additions to the Shakespearean repertory, until only six Shakespearean dramas were left unrepresented, viz.—*Richard II.,* the three parts of *Henry VI., Troilus and Cressida,* and *Titus Andronicus.* Of these, one alone, *Richard II.,* is really actable.

The leading principles, to which Phelps strictly

adhered throughout his career of management, call
for most careful consideration. He gathered round
him a company of actors and actresses, whom he
zealously trained to interpret Shakespeare's language.
He accustomed his colleagues to act harmoniously
together, and to sacrifice to the welfare of the whole
enterprise pretensions to individual prominence.
No long continuous run of any one piece was permitted by the rules of the playhouse. The programme was constantly changed. The scenic appliances were simple, adequate, and inexpensive.
The supernumerary staff was restricted to the
smallest practicable number. The general expenses
were consequently kept within narrow limits. For
every thousand pounds that Charles Kean laid out
at the Princess's Theatre on scenery and other expenses of production, Phelps in his most ornate revivals spent less than a fourth of that sum. For
the pounds spent by managers on more recent
revivals, Phelps would have spent only as many
shillings. In the result, Phelps reaped from the
profits of his efforts a handsome unencumbered income. During the same period Charles Kean grew
more and more deeply involved in oppressive debt,
and at a later date Sir Henry Irving made over to
the public a hundred thousand pounds above his
receipts.

VI

Why, then, should not Phelps's encouraging
experiment be made again ? [1]

[1] It is just to notice, among endeavours of the late years of the
past century, to which I confine my remarks here, the efforts to
produce Shakespearean drama worthily which were made by

Before anyone may commit himself to an affirmative reply, it is needful for him to realise fully the precise demands which a system like that of Phelps makes, when rightly interpreted, on the character, ability, and energy of the actors and actresses. If scenery in Shakespearean productions be relegated to its proper place in the background of the stage, it is necessary that the acting, from top to bottom of the cast, shall be more efficient and better harmonised than that which is commonly associated with spectacular representations. The simple method of producing Shakespeare focusses the interest of the audience on the actor and actress; it gives them a dignity and importance which are unknown to the complex method. Under the latter system, the attention of the spectator is largely absorbed by the triumphs of the scene-painter and machinist, of the costumier and the musicians. The actor and actress often elude notice altogether.

Charles Alexander Calvert at the Prince's Theatre, Manchester, between 1864 and 1874. Calvert, who was a warm admirer of Phelps, attempted to blend Phelps's method with Charles Kean's, and bestowed great scenic elaboration on the production of at least eight plays of Shakespeare. Financially the speculation saw every vicissitude, and Calvert's experience may be quoted in support of the view that a return to Phelps's method is financially safer than a return to Charles Kean's. More recently the Elizabethan Stage Society endeavoured to produce, with a simplicity which erred on the side of severity, many plays of Shakespeare and other literary dramas. No scenery was employed, and the performers were dressed in Elizabethan costume. The Society's work was done privately, and did not invite any genuine test of publicity. The representation by the Society on November 11, 1899, in the Lecture Theatre at Burlington House, of *Richard II.*, in which Mr Granville Barker played the King with great charm and judgment, showed the fascination that a competent rendering of Shakespeare's text exerts, even in the total absence of scenery, over a large audience of suitable temper.

Macready, whose theatrical career was anterior to the modern spectacular period of Shakespearean representation, has left on record a deliberate opinion of Charles Kean's elaborate methods at the Princess's Theatre in their relation to drama and the histrionic art. Macready's verdict has an universal application. "The production of the Shakespearean plays at the Princess's Theatre," the great actor wrote to Lady Pollock on the 1st of May, 1859, rendered the spoken text "more like a running commentary on the spectacles exhibited than the scenic arrangements an illustration of the text." No criticism could define more convincingly the humiliation to which the author's words are exposed by spectacle, or, what is more pertinent to the immediate argument, the evil which is worked by spectacle on the actor.

Acting can be, and commonly tends to be, the most mechanical of physical exercises. The actor is often a mere automaton who repeats night after night the same unimpressive trick of voice, eye, and gesture. His defects of understanding may be comparatively unobtrusive in a spectacular display, where he is liable to escape censure by escaping observation, or at best to be regarded as a showman. Furthermore, the long runs which scenic excess brings in its train accentuate the mechanical actor's imperfections and diminish his opportunities of remedying them. On the other hand, acting can rise in opposite conditions into the noblest of the arts. The great actor relies for genuine success on no mere gesticulatory mechanism. Imaginative insight, passion, the gift of oratory, grace and dignity of movement and bearing, perfect command of the voice in the whole gamut of its inflections are the constituent qualities of true histrionic capacity.

In no drama are these qualities more necessary, or are ampler opportunities offered for their use, than in the plays of Shakespeare. Not only in the leading rôles of his masterpieces, but in the subordinate parts throughout the range of his work, the highest abilities of the actor or actress can find some scope for employment. It is therefore indispensable that the standard of Shakespearean acting should always be maintained at the highest level, if Shakespearean drama is to be fitly rendered in the theatre. The worst of the evils, which are inherent in scenic excess, with its accompaniment of long runs, is its tendency to sanction the maintenance of the level of acting at something below the highest. Phelps was keenly alive to this peril, and his best energies were devoted to training his actors and actresses for all the rôles in the cast, great and small. Actors and actresses of the first rank on occasion filled minor parts, in order to heighten the efficiency of the presentation. Actors and actresses who have the dignity of their profession at heart might be expected to welcome the revival of a system which alone guarantees their talent and the work of the dramatist due recognition, even if it leave histrionic incompetence no hope of escape from the scorn that befits it. It is on the aspiration and sentiment of the acting profession that must largely depend the final answer to the question whether Phelps's experiment can be made again with likelihood of success.

VII

Foreign experience tells in favour of the contention that, if Shakespeare's plays are to be honoured on the modern stage as they deserve, they must be freed of the existing incubus of scenic machinery. French acting has always won and deserved admiration. There is no doubt that one cause of its permanently high repute is the absolute divorce in the French theatre of drama from spectacle.

Molière stands to French literature in much the same relation as Shakespeare stands to English literature. Molière's plays are constantly acted in French theatres with a scenic austerity which is unknown to the humblest of our theatres. A French audience would regard it as sacrilege to convert a comedy of Molière into a spectacle. The French people are commonly credited with a love of ornament and display to which the English people are assumed to be strangers, but their treatment of Molière is convincing proof that their artistic sense is ultimately truer than our own.

The mode of producing Shakespeare on the stage in Germany supplies an argument to the same effect. In Berlin and Vienna, and in all the chief towns of German-speaking Europe, Shakespeare's plays are produced constantly and in all their variety, for the most part, in conditions which are directly anti-thetical to those prevailing in the West-end theatres of London. Twenty-eight of Shakespeare's thirty-seven plays figure in the répertoires of the leading companies of German-speaking actors.

The currently accepted method of presentation can be judged from the following personal experience.

A few years ago I was in the Burg-Theater in Vienna
on a Sunday night—the night on which the great
working population of Vienna chiefly take their
recreation, as in this country it is chiefly taken by
the great working population on Saturday night.
The Burg-Theater in Vienna is one of the largest
theatres in the world. It is of similar dimensions to
Drury Lane Theatre or Covent Garden Opera-
house. On the occasion of my visit the play produced was Shakespeare's *Antony and Cleopatra*.
The house was crowded in every part. The scenic
arrangements were simple and unobtrusive, but
were well calculated to suggest the Oriental atmosphere of the plot. There was no music before the
performance, or during the intervals between the
acts, or as an accompaniment to great speeches in
the progress of the play. There was no making
love, nor any dying to slow music, although the
stage directions were followed scrupulously ; the
song "Come, thou Monarch of the Vine," was sung
to music in the drinking scene on board Pompey's
galley, and there were the appointed flourishes of
trumpets and drums. The acting was competent,
though not of the highest calibre, but a satisfactory
level was evenly maintained throughout the cast.
There were no conspicuous deflections from the
adequate standard. The character of whom I have
the most distinct recollection was Enobarbus, the
level-headed and straight-hitting critic of the action
—a comparatively subordinate part, which was
filled by one of the most distinguished actors of the
Viennese stage. He fitted his part with telling
accuracy.

The whole piece was listened to with breathless

interest. It was acted practically without curtailment, and, although the performance lasted nearly
five hours, no sign of impatience manifested itself
at any point. This was no exceptional experience
at the Burg-Theater. Plays of Shakespeare are
acted there repeatedly—on an average twice a
week—and, I am credibly informed, with identical
results to those of which I was an eye-witness.

VIII

It cannot be flattering to our self-esteem that the
Austrian people should show a greater and a wiser
appreciation of the theatrical capacities of Shakespeare's masterpieces than we who are Shakespeare's
countrymen and the most direct and rightful heirs of
his glorious achievements. How is the disturbing
fact to be accounted for? Is it possible that it is
attributable to some decay in us of the imagination—to a growing slowness on our part to appreciate works of imagination? When one reflects
on the simple mechanical contrivances which satisfied the theatrical audiences, not only of Shakespeare's own day, but of the eighteenth century,
during which Shakespeare was repeatedly performed; when one compares the simplicity of scenic
mechanism in the past with its complexity in our
own time, one can hardly resist the conclusion that
the imagination of the theatre-going public is no
longer what it was of old. The play alone was
then "the thing." Now "the thing," it seems, is
something outside the play—namely, the painted
scene or the costume, the music or the dance.

Garrick played Macbeth in an ordinary Court suit of his own era. The habiliments proper to Celtic monarchs of the eleventh century were left to be supplied by the imagination of the spectators or not at all. No realistic "effects" helped the play forward in Garrick's time, yet the attention of his audience, the critics tell us, was never known to stray when he produced a great play by Shakespeare. In Shakespeare's day boys or men took the part of women, and how characters like Lady Macbeth and Desdemona were adequately rendered by youths beggars belief. But renderings in such conditions proved popular and satisfactory. Such a fact seems convincing testimony, not to the ability of Elizabethan or Jacobean boys—the nature of boys is a pretty permanent factor in human society —but to the superior imaginative faculty of adult Elizabethan or Jacobean playgoers, in whom, as in Garrick's time, the needful dramatic illusion was far more easily evoked than it is nowadays.

This is no exhilarating conclusion. But less exhilarating is the endeavour that is sometimes made by advocates of the system of spectacle to prove that Shakespeare himself would have appreciated the modern developments of the scenic art— nay, more, that he himself has justified them. This line of argument serves to confirm the suggested defect of imagination in the present generation. The well-known chorus before the first act of *Henry V.* is the evidence which is relied upon to show that Shakespeare wished his plays to be, in journalistic dialect, "magnificently staged," and that he deplored the inability of his uncouth age to realise that wish. The lines are familiar; but it is necessary to quote them at length, in fairness to those who judge them to be a defence of the spectacular principle in the presentation of Shakespearean drama. They run:—

> O for a muse of fire, that would ascend
> The brightest heaven of invention,
> A kingdom for a stage, princes to act,
> And monarchs to behold the swelling scene!
> Then should the warlike Harry, like himself,
> Assume the port of Mars; and at his heels,
> Leash'd in like hounds, should famine, sword and fire
> Crouch for employment. But pardon, gentles all,
> The flat unraised spirits that have dar'd
> On this unworthy scaffold to bring forth
> So great an object: can this cockpit hold
> The vasty fields of France? or may we cram
> Within this wooden O the very casques
> That did affright the air at Agincourt?
> O, pardon! since a crooked figure may
> Attest in little place a million;
> And let us, ciphers to this great accompt,
> On your imaginary forces work.
> Suppose within the girdle of these walls
> Are now confined two mighty monarchies,
> Whose high upreared and abutting fronts,
> The perilous narrow ocean parts asunder;
> Piece out our imperfections with your thoughts;
> Into a thousand parts divide one man,
> And make imaginary puissance:
> Think, when we talk of horses, that you see them
> Printing their proud hoofs i' the receiving earth.
> For 'tis your thoughts that now must deck our kings,
> Carry them here and there, jumping o'er times,
> Turning the accomplishment of many years
> Into an hour glass.

There is, in my opinion, no strict relevance in these lines to the enquiry whether Shakespeare's work should be treated on the stage as drama or spectacle. Nay, I go further, and assert that, as far as the speech touches the question at issue at all, it tells against the pretensions of spectacle.

Shortly stated, Shakespeare's splendid prelude to his play of *Henry V.* is a spirited appeal to his audience not to waste regrets on defects of stage machinery, but to bring to the observation of his piece their highest powers of imagination, whereby alone can full justice be done to a majestic theme. The central topic of the choric speech is the essential limitations of all scenic appliances.   The dramatist reminds us that the literal presentation of life itself, in all its movement and action, lies outside the range of the stage, especially the movement and action of life in its most glorious manifestations, Obvious conditions of space do not allow "two mighty monarchies" literally to be confined within the walls of a theatre.   Obvious conditions of time cannot turn "the accomplishments of many years into an hour glass."   Shakespeare is airing no private grievance.   He is not complaining that his plays were in his own day inadequately upholstered in the theatre, or that the "scaffold" on which they were produced was "unworthy" of them.   The words have no concern with the contention that modern upholstery and spectacular machinery render Shakespeare's play a justice which was denied them in his lifetime.   As reasonably one might affirm that the modern theatre has now conquered the ordinary conditions of time and space; that a modern playhouse can, if the manager so will it, actually hold within its walls the "vasty fields of France," or confine "two mighty monarchies."

A wider and quite impersonal trend of thought is offered for consideration by Shakespeare's majestic eloquence. The dramatist bids us bear in mind that his lines do no more than suggest the things he would have the audience see and understand; the actors aid the suggestion according to their ability. But the crucial point of the utterance is the warning that the illusion of the drama can only be rendered complete in the theatre by the working of the "imaginary forces" of the spectators. It is needful for them to "make imaginary puissance," if the play is to triumph. It is their "thoughts" that "must deck" the kings of the stage, if the dramatist's meaning is to get home. The poet modestly underestimated the supreme force of his own imaginative genius when giving these admonitions to his hearers. But they are warnings of universal application, and can never be safely ignored.

Such an exordium as the chorus before *Henry V.* would indeed be pertinent to every stage performance of great drama in any age or country. It matters not whether the spectacular machinery be of royal magnificence or of poverty-stricken squalor. Let us make the extravagant assumption that all the artistic genius in the world and all the treasure in the Bank of England were placed at the command of the theatrical manager in order to enable him to produce a great play on his stage supremely well from his own scenic point of view. Even then it would not be either superfluous or impertinent for the manager to adjure the audience to piece out the "imperfections" of the scenery with their "thoughts" or imagination. The spectator's "imaginary puissance" is, practically in every circumstance, the key-stone of the dramatic illusion.

The only conditions in which Shakespeare's adjuration would be superfluous or impertinent would accompany the presentment in the theatre of some circumscribed incident of life which is capable of so literal a rendering as to leave no room for any make-believe or illusion at all. The unintellectual playgoer, to whom Shakespeare will never really prove attractive in any guise, has little or no imagination to exercise, and he only tolerates a performance in the theatre when little or no demand is made on the exercise of the imaginative faculty. "The groundlings," said Shakespeare for all time, "are capable of [appreciating] nothing but inexplicable dumb shows and noise." They would be hugely delighted nowadays with a scene in which two real motor cars, with genuine chauffeurs and passengers, raced uproariously across the stage. That is realism in its nakedness. That is realism reduced to its first principles. Realistic "effects," however speciously beautiful they may be, invariably tend to realism of that primal type, which satisfies the predilections of the groundling, and reduces drama to the level of the cinematograph.

IX

The deliberate pursuit of scenic realism is antagonistic to the ultimate law of dramatic art. In the case of great plays, the dramatic representation is most successful from the genuinely artistic point of view—which is the only point of view worthy of discussion—when the just dramatic illusion is produced by simple and unpretending scenic appliances, in which the inevitable "imperfections" are frankly left to be supplied by the "thoughts" or imagination of the spectators.

Lovers of Shakespeare should lose no opportunity of urging the cause of simplicity in the production of the plays of Shakespeare. Practical common-sense, practical considerations of a pecuniary kind, teach us that it is only by the adoption of simple methods of production that we can hope to have Shakespeare represented in our theatres constantly and in all his variety. Until Shakespeare is represented thus, the spiritual and intellectual enlightenment, which his achievement offers English-speaking people will remain wholly inaccessible to the majority who do not read him, and will be only in part at the command of the few who do. Nay, more: until Shakespeare is represented on the stage constantly and in his variety, English-speaking men and women are liable to the imputation, not merely of failing in the homage due to the greatest of their countrymen, but of falling short of their neighbours in Germany and Austria in the capacity of appreciating supremely great imaginative literature.

II

SHAKESPEARE AND THE ELIZABETHAN PLAYGOER [1]

I

IN a freak of fancy, Robert Louis Stevenson sent to a congenial spirit the imaginary intelligence that a well-known firm of London publishers had, after their wont, "declined with thanks" six undiscovered tragedies, one romantic comedy, a fragment of a journal extending over six years, and an unfinished autobiography reaching up to the first performance of *King John* by "that venerable but still respected writer, William Shakespeare." Stevenson was writing in a frivolous mood; but such words stir the imagination. The ordinary person, if he had to choose among the enumerated items of Shakespeare's newly-discovered manuscripts, would cheerfully go without the six new tragedies and the one romantic comedy, if he had at his disposal, by way of consolation, the journal extending over six years and the autobiography

[1] This paper, which was first printed in " An English Miscellany, presented to Dr Furnivall in honour of his seventy-fifth birthday " (Oxford: At the Clarendon Press, 1901), was written as a lecture for delivery on Tuesday afternoon, March 20, 1900, at Queen's College (for women) in Harley Street, London, in aid of the Fund for securing a picture commemorating Queen Victoria's visit to the College in 1898.

reaching up to the first performance of *King John*. We should deem ourselves fortunate if we had the journal alone. It would hardly matter which six years of Shakespeare's life the journal covered. As a boy, as a young actor, as an industrious reviser of other men's plays, as the humorous creator of Falstaff, Benedick, and Mercutio, as the profound "natural philosopher" of the great tragedies, he could never have been quite an ordinary diarist. Great men have been known to keep diaries in which the level of interest does not rise above a visit to the barber or the dentist. The common routine of life interested Shakespeare, but something beyond it must have found place in his journal. Reference to his glorious achievement must have gained entry there.

Some notice, we may be sure, figured in Shakespeare's diary of the first performances of his great plays on the stage. However eminent a man is through native genius or from place of power, he can never be indifferent, whatever his casual professions to the contrary, to the reception accorded by his fellowmen to the work of his hand and head. I picture Shakespeare as the soul of modesty and gentleness in the social relations of life, avoiding unbecoming self-advertisement, and rating at its just value empty flattery, the mere adulation of the lips. Gushing laudation is as little to the taste of wise men as treacle. They cannot escape condiments of the kind, but the smaller and less frequent the doses the more they are content. Shakespeare no doubt had the great man's self-confidence which renders him to a large extent independent of the opinion of his fellows. At the same

time, the knowledge that he had succeeded in
stirring the reader or hearer of his plays, the knowledge that his words had gripped their hearts and
intellects, cannot have been ungrateful to him. To
desire recognition for his work is for the artist an
inevitable and a laudable ambition. A working
dramatist by the circumstance of his calling appeals as soon as the play is written to the playgoer for a sympathetic appreciation. Nature im-
pelled Shakespeare to note on the pages of his
journal his impression of the sentiment with which
the fruits of his pen were welcomed in the playhouse.

But Shakespeare's journal does not exist, and
we can only speculate as to its contents.

II

We would give much to know how Shakespeare
recorded in his diary the first performance of
Hamlet, the most fascinating of all his works. He
himself, we are credibly told, played the Ghost.
We would give much for a record of the feelings
which lay on the first production of the play beneath
the breast of the silent apparition in the first scene
which twice crossed the stage and affrighted Mar-
cellus, Horatio, and the guards on the platform
before the castle of Elsinore. No piece of literature that ever came from human pen or brain is
more closely packed with fruit of the imaginative
study of human life than is Shakespeare's tragedy
of *Hamlet;* and while the author acted the part of
the Ghost in the play's initial representation in

the theatre, he was watching the revelation of his
pregnant message for the first time to the external
world. When the author in his weird rôle of Hamlet's murdered father opened his lips for the first
time, we might almost imagine that in the words
"pity me not, but lend thy serious hearing to what
I shall unfold," he was reflecting the author's personal interest in the proceedings of that memorable
afternoon.[1] We can imagine Shakespeare, as he
saw the audience responding to his grave appeal,
giving with a growing confidence, the subsequent
words which he repeated while he moved to the
centre of the platform-stage, and turned to face the
whole house:—

> I find thee apt;
> And duller shouldst thou be than the fat weed
> That rots itself in ease on Lethe wharf,
> Wouldst thou not stir in this.

As the Ghost vanished and the air rang mysteri-
ously with his piercing words "Remember me,"
we would like to imagine the whole intelligence of
Elizabethan England responding to that cry as it
sprang on its first utterance in the theatre from the
great dramatist's own lips. Since that memorable
day, at any rate, the whole intelligence of the
world has responded to that cry with all Hamlet's
ecstasy, and with but a single modification of the
phraseology:—

> Remember thee!
> Ay, thou *great soul*, while memory holds a seat
> In this distracted globe.

---

[1] Performances of plays in Shakespeare's time always took
place in the afternoon.

III

There is a certain justification, in fact, for the fancy that the *plaudites* were loud and long, when Shakespeare created the rôle of the "poor ghost" in the first production of his play of *Hamlet* in 1602. There is no doubt at all that Shakespeare conspicuously caught the ear of the Elizabethan playgoer at a very early date in his career, and that he held it firmly for life. "These plays," wrote two of his professional associates of the reception of the whole series in the playhouse in his lifetime —"These plays have had their trial already, and stood out all appeals." Matthew Arnold, apparently quite unconsciously, echoed the precise phrase when seeking to express poetically, the universality of Shakespeare's reputation in our own day.

Others abide our judgment, thou art free,

is the first line of Arnold's well-known sonnet, which attests the rank allotted to Shakespeare in the literary hierarchy by the professional critic, nearly two and a half centuries after the dramatist's death. There was no narrower qualification in the apostrophe of Shakespeare by Ben Jonson, a very critical contemporary, as:—

Soul of *the age*,
The applause, delight, and wonder of *our stage*.

This play of *Hamlet*, this play of his "which most kindled English hearts," received a specially enthusiastic welcome from Elizabethan playgoers. It was acted within its first year of production repeatedly ("divers times"), not merely in London "and elsewhere," but also—an unusual distinction

—at the Universities of Oxford and Cambridge. It was reprinted four times within eight years of its birth.

Thus the charge sometimes brought against the Elizabethan playgoer of failing to recognise Shakespeare's sovereign genius should be reckoned among popular errors. It was not merely the recognition of the critical and highly educated that Shakespeare received in person. It was by the voice of the half-educated populace, whose heart and intellect were for once in the right, that he was acclaimed the greatest interpreter of human nature that literature had known, and, as subsequent experience has proved, was likely to know. There is evidence that throughout his lifetime and for a generation afterwards his plays drew crowds to pit, boxes, and gallery alike. It is true that he was one of a number of popular dramatists, many of whom had rare gifts, and all of whom glowed with a spark of the genuine literary fire. But Shakespeare was the sun in the firmament: when his light shone, the fires of all contemporaries paled in the contemporary playgoer's eye. There is forcible and humorous portrayal of human frailty and eccentricity in plays of Shakespeare's contemporary, Ben Jonson. Ben Jonson was a classical scholar, which Shakespeare was not. Jonson was as well versed in Roman history as a college tutor. But when Shakespeare and Ben Jonson both tried their hands at dramatising episodes in Roman history, the Elizabethan public of all degrees of intelligence welcomed Shakespeare's efforts with an enthusiasm which they rigidly withheld from Ben Jonson's. This is how an ordinary playgoer con-

trasted the reception of Jonson's Roman play of
Catiline's Conspiracy with that of Shakespeare's
Roman play of *Julius Cæsar:*—

> So have I seen when Cæsar would appear,
> And on the stage at half-sword parley were
> Brutus and Cassius—oh! how the audience
> Were ravished, with what wonder they went thence;
> When some new day they would not brook a line
> Of tedious though well-laboured Catiline.

Shakespeare was the popular favourite. It is
rare that the artist who is a hero with the multitude
is also a hero with the cultivated few. But Shakespeare's universality of appeal was such as to include
among his worshippers from the first the trained
and the untrained playgoer of his time.

IV

Very early in his career did Shakespeare attract
the notice of the cultivated section of Elizabeth's
Court, and hardly sufficient notice has been taken
by students of the poet's biography of the earliest
recognition accorded him by the great queen, herself an inveterate lover of the 'drama, and an embodiment of the taste of the people in literature.
The story is worth retelling. In the middle of December 1594, Queen Elizabeth removed from Whitehall to Greenwich to spend Christmas at that palace
of Greenwich in which she was born sixty-one years
earlier. And she made the celebration of Christmas
of 1594 more memorable than any other in the
annals of her reign or in the literary history of the
country by summoning Shakespeare to Court. It
was less than eight years since the poet had first set
foot in the metropolis. His career was little more

than opened. But by 1594 Shakespeare had given his countrymen unmistakable indications of the stuff of which he was made. His progress had been more sure than rapid. A young man of two-and-twenty, burdened with a wife and three children, he had left his home in the little country town of Stratford-on-Avon in 1586 to seek his fortune in London. Without friends, without money, he had, like any other stage-struck youth, set his heart on becoming an actor in the metropolis. Fortune favoured him. He sought and won the humble office of call-boy in a London playhouse; but no sooner had his foot touched the lowest rung of the theatrical ladder than his genius taught him that the topmost rung was within his reach. He tried his hand on the revision of an old play, and the manager was not slow to recognise an unmatched gift for dramatic writing.

It was probably not till 1591, when Shakespeare was twenty-seven, that his earliest original play, *Love's Labour's Lost*, was performed. It showed the hand of a beginner; it abounded in trivial witticisms. But above all, there shone out clearly and unmistakably the dramatic and poetic fire, the humorous outlook on life, the insight into human feeling, which were to inspire Titanic achievements in the future.

Soon after, Shakespeare scaled the tragic heights of *Romeo and Juliet*, and he was hailed as the prophet of a new world of art. Fashionable London society then, as now, befriended the theatre. Cultivated noblemen offered their patronage to promising writers for the stage, and Shakespeare soon gained the ear of the young Earl of Southampton, one of the most accomplished and handsome of the queen's noble courtiers, who was said to spend nearly all his time in going to the playhouse every day. It was at Southampton's suggestion, that, in the week preceding the Christmas of 1594, the Lord Chamberlain sent word to The Theatre in Shoreditch, where Shakespeare was at work as playwright and actor, that the poet was expected at Court on two days following Christmas, in order to give his sovereign on the two evenings a taste of his quality. He was to act before her in his own plays.

It cannot have been Shakespeare's promise as an actor that led to the royal summons. His histrionic fame had not progressed at the same rate as his literary repute. He was never to win the laurels of a great actor. His most conspicuous triumph on the stage was achieved in middle life as the Ghost in his own *Hamlet*, and he ordinarily confined his efforts to old men of secondary rank. Ample compensation was provided by his companions for his personal deficiencies as an actor on his first visit to Court; he was to come supported by actors of the highest eminence in their generation. Directions were given that the greatest of the tragic actors of the day, Richard Burbage, and the greatest of the comic actors, William Kemp, were to bear the young actor-dramatist company. With neither of these was Shakespeare's histrionic position then or at any time comparable. For years they were leaders of the acting profession.

Shakespeare's relations with Burbage and Kemp were close, both privately and professionally. Almost all Shakespeare's great tragic characters were created on the stage by Burbage, who had lately roused London to enthusiasm by his stirring presen-

tation of Shakespeare's *Richard III.* for the first
time. As long as Kemp lived, he conferred a like
service on many of Shakespeare's comic characters;
and he had recently proved his worth as a Shakespearean comedian by his original rendering of the
part of Peter, the Nurse's graceless attendant, in
Romeo and Juliet. Thus stoutly backed, Shakespeare appeared for the first time in the royal pres-
ence-chamber of Greenwich Palace on the evening
of St. Stephen's Day (the Boxing Day of subsequent generations) in 1594.

Extant documentary evidence attests that Shakespeare and his two associates performed one "comedy
or interlude" on that night of Boxing Day in 1594,
and gave another "comedy or interlude" on the
next night but one; that the Lord Chamberlain paid
the three men for their services the sum of £13, 6s.
8d., and that the queen added to the honorarium,
as a personal proof of her satisfaction, the further
sum of £6, 13s. 4d. These were substantial sums
in those days, when the purchasing power of money
was eight times as much as it is to-day, and the
three actors' reward would now be equivalent to
£160.

Unhappily the record does not go beyond the
payment of the money. What words of commendation or encouragement Shakespeare received from
his royal auditor are not handed down, nor do we
know for certain what plays were performed on the
great occasion. All the scenes came from Shakespeare's repertory, and it is reasonable to infer that
they were drawn from *Love's Labour's Lost*, which
was always popular in later years at Elizabeth's
Court, and from *The Comedy of Errors*, where the

farcial confusions and horse-play were after the
queen's own heart and robust taste. But nothing
can be stated with absolute certainty except that
on December 29 Shakespeare travelled up the river
from Greenwich to London with a heavier purse
and a lighter heart than on his setting out. That
the visit had in all ways been crowned with success
there is ample indirect evidence. He and his work
had fascinated his sovereign, and many a time
during her remaining nine years of life was she to
seek delight again in the renderings of plays by
himself and his fellow-actors at her palaces on the
banks of the Thames. When Shakespeare was
penning his new play of *A Midsummer Night's
Dream* next year, he could not forbear to make a
passing obeisance of gallantry (in that vein for
which the old spinster queen was always thirsting)
to "a fair vestal throned by the West," who passed
her life "in maiden meditation, fancy free."

Although literature and art can flourish without
royal favour and royal patronage, still it is rare that
royal patronage has any other effect than that of
raising those who are its objects in the estimation
of contemporaries. The interest that Shakespeare's
work excited at Court was continuous throughout
his life. When James I. ascended the throne,
no author was more frequently honoured by
"command" performances of his plays in the
presence of the sovereign. And then, as now,
the playgoer's appreciation was quickened by his
knowledge that the play they were witnessing had
been produced before the Court at Whitehall a few
days earlier. Shakespeare's publishers were not
above advertising facts like these, as may be seen by

a survey of the title-pages of editions published in his life-time. "The pleasant conceited comedy called *Love's Labour's Lost*" was advertised with the appended words, "as it was presented before her highness this last Christmas." "A most pleasant and excellent conceited comedy of *Sir John Falstaff and the Merry Wives of Windsor*" was stated to have been "divers times acted both before her majesty and elsewhere." The great play of *Lear* was advertised, "as it was played before the king's majesty at Whitehall on St. Stephen's night in the Christmas holidays."

V

Although Shakespeare's illimitable command of expression, his universality of knowledge and insight, cannot easily be overlooked by any man or woman of ordinary human faculty, still, from some points of view, there is ground for surprise that the Elizabethan playgoer's enthusiasm for Shakespeare's work was so marked and unequivocal as we know that it was.

Let us consider for a moment the physical conditions of the theatre, the methods of stage representation, in Shakespeare's day. Theatres were in their infancy. The theatre was a new institution in social life for Shakespeare's public, and the whole system of the theatrical world came into being after Shakespeare came into the world. In estimating Shakespeare's genius one ought to bear in mind that he was a pioneer—almost the creator or first designer—of English drama, as well as the practised workman in unmatched perfection. There were before his day some efforts made at dramatic representation. The Middle Ages had their miracle plays and moralities and interludes. But of poetic, literary, romantic drama, England knew nothing until Shakespeare was of age. Marlowe, who in his early years inaugurated English tragedy, was Shakespeare's senior by only two months. It was not till 1576, when Shakespeare was twelve, that London for the first time possessed a theatre—a building definitely built for the purpose of presenting plays. Before that year inn-yards or platforms, which were improvised in market-places or fields, served for the performance of interludes or moralities.

Nor was it precisely in London proper that this primal theatre, which is known in history simply as The Theatre, was set up. London in Shakespeare's day was a small town, barely a mile square, with a population little exceeding 60,000 persons. Within the circuit of the city-walls vacant spaces were sparse, and public opinion deprecated the erection of buildings upon them. Moreover, the puritan clergy and their pious flocks, who constituted an active section of the citizens, were inclined to resist the conversion of any existing building into such a Satanic trap for unwary souls as they believed a playhouse of necessity to be.

It was, accordingly, in the fields near London, not in London itself, that the first theatre was set up. Adjoining the city lay pleasant meadows, which were bright in spring-time with daisies and violets. Green lanes conducted the wayfarer to the rural retreat of Islington, and citizens went for change of air to the rustic seclusion of Maryle-bone. A site for the first-born of London playhouses was chosen in the spacious fields of Finsbury and Shoreditch, which the Great Eastern Railway now occupies. The innovation of a theatre, even though it were placed outside the walls of the city, excited serious misgiving among the godly minority. But, after much controversy the battle was finally won by the supporters of the play, and The Theatre was launched on a prosperous career. Two or three other theatres quickly sprang up in neighbouring parts of London's environment. When Shakespeare was reaching the zenith of his career, the centre of theatrical life was transferred from Shoreditch to the Southwark bank of the river Thames, at the south side of London Bridge, which lay outside the city's boundaries, but was easy of access to residents within them. It was at the Globe Theatre on Bankside, which was reached by bridge or by boat from the city-side of the river, that Shakespearean drama won its most glorious triumphs.

VI

Despite the gloomy warnings of the preachers, the new London theatres had for the average Elizabethan all the fascination that a new toy has for a child. The average Elizabethan repudiated the jeremiads of the ultra-pious, and instantaneously became an enthusiastic playgoer. During the last year of the sixteenth century, an intelligent visitor to London, Thomas Platter, a native of Basle, whose journal has recently been discovered,[1] de-

[1] Professor Binz of Basle printed in September, 1899, some extracts from Thomas Platter's unpublished diary of travels under the title: *Londoner Theater und Schauspiele im Jahre* 1599. Platter spent a month in London—September 18 to October 20, 1599. Platter's manuscript is in the Library of Basle University.

scribed with ingenuous sympathy the delight which the populace displayed in the new playhouses.

Some attractions which the theatres offered had little concern with the drama. Their advantages included the privileges of eating and drinking while the play was in progress. After the play there was invariably a dance on the stage, often a brisk and boisterous Irish jig.

Other features of the entertainment seem to have been less exhilarating. The mass of the spectators filled the pit, where there was standing room only; there were no seats. The admission rarely cost more than a penny; but there was no roof. The rain beat at pleasure on the heads of the "penny" auditors; while pickpockets commonly plied their trade among them without much hindrance when the piece absorbed the attention of the "house." Seats or benches were only to be found in the two galleries, the larger portions of which were separated into "rooms" or boxes; prices there ranged from twopence to half-a-crown. If the playgoer had plenty of money at his command he could, according to the German visitor, hire not only a seat but a cushion to elevate his stature; "so that," says our author, "he might not only see the play, but"—what is also often more important for rich people—"be seen" by the audience to be occupying a specially distinguished place. Fashionable playgoers of the male sex might, if they opened their purses wide enough, occupy stools on the wide platform-stage. Such a practice proved embarrassing, not only to the performers, but to those who had to content themselves with the penny pit. Standing in front and by the sides of the projecting stage, they could often only catch glimpses of the actors through chinks in serried ranks of stools.

The histrionic and scenic conditions, in which Shakespeare's plays were originally produced, present a further series of disadvantages which, from any modern point of view, render the more amazing the unqualified enthusiasm of the Elizabethan playgoer.

There was no scenery, although there were crude endeavours to create scenic illusion by means of "properties" like rocks, tombs, caves, trees, tables, chairs, and pasteboard dishes of food. There was at the outset no music, save flourishes on trumpets at the opening of the play and between the acts. The scenes within each act were played continuously without pause. The bare boards of the platform-stage, which no proscenium nor curtain darkened, projected so far into the auditorium, that the actors spoke in the very centre of the house. Trapdoors were in use for the entrance of "ghosts" and other mysterious personages. At the back of the stage was a raised platform or balcony, from which often hung loose curtains; through them the actors passed to the forepart of the stage. The balcony was pressed into the service when the text of the play indicated that the speakers were not actually standing on the same level. From the raised platform Juliet addressed Romeo in the balcony scene, and the citizens of Angers in *King John* held colloquy with the English besiegers. This was, indeed, almost the furthest limit of the Elizabethan stage - manager's notion of scenic realism. The boards, which were bare save for the occasional presence of rough properties, were held to present

adequate semblance, as the play demanded, of a
king's throne-room, a chapel, a forest, a ship at sea,
a mountainous pass, a market-place, a battle-field,
or a churchyard.

The costumes had no pretensions to fit the
period or place of the action. They were the
ordinary dresses of various classes of the day, but
were often of rich material, and in the height of
the current fashion. False hair and beards, crowns
and sceptres, mitres and croziers, armour, helmets,
shields, vizors, and weapons of war, hoods, bands,
and cassocks, were mainly relied on to indicate
among the characters differences of rank or profession.

The foreign observer, Thomas Platter of Basle,
was impressed by the splendour of the actors'
costumes. He accounted for it in a manner that
negatives any suggestion of dramatic propriety:—

"The players wear the most costly and beautiful dresses, for it is the custom in England, that
when noblemen or knights die, they leave their
finest clothes to their servants, who, since it would
not be fitting for them to wear such splendid gar-
ments, sell them soon afterwards to the players for
a small sum."

The most striking defect in the practice of the
Elizabethan playhouse, according to accepted notions, lies in the allotment of the female rôles. It
was thought unseemly for women to act at all.
Female parts were played by boys or men—a substitution lacking, from the modern point of view, in
grace and seemliness. But the standard of propriety in such matters varies from age to age.
Shakespeare alludes quite complacently to the ap-

pearance of boys and men in women's parts. He
makes Rosalind say, laughingly and saucily, to the
men of the audience in the epilogue to *As You Like
It*, "If I were a woman I would kiss as many of you
as had beards that pleased me." "*If I were* a
woman," she says. The jest lies in the fact that
the speaker was not a woman but a boy. Similarly,
Cleopatra on her downfall in *Antony and Cleopatra*,
(V. ii. 220), laments

> the quick comedians
> Extemporally will stage us . . . and I shall see
> Some squeaking Cleopatra *boy* my greatness.

The experiment of entrusting a boy with the
part of Ophelia was lately tried in London not
unsuccessfully; but it is difficult to realise how
a boy or young man could adequately interpret
most of Shakespeare's female characters. It seems
almost sacrilegious to conceive the part of Cleopatra, the most highly sensitised in its minutest
details of all dramatic portrayals of female character,—it seems almost sacrilegious to submit Cleopatra's sublimity of passion for interpretation by
an unfledged representative of the other sex. Yet
such solecisms were imperative under the theatrical
system of the late sixteenth and early seventeenth
century. Men taking women's parts seem to have
worn masks, but that can hardly have improved
matters. Flute, when he complains that it would
hardly befit him to play a woman's part because
he had a beard coming, is bidden by his resourceful
manager, Quince, play Thisbe in a "mask." At
times actors who had long lost the roses of youth
masqueraded in women's rôles. Thereby the un-
gainliness which marked the distribution of the

cast in Elizabethan and Jacobean playhouses was
often forced into stronger light.

It was not till the seventeenth century was well
advanced that women were permitted to act in
public theatres. Then the gracelessness of the
masculine method was acknowledged and deplored.
It was the character of Desdemona which was first
undertaken by a woman, and the absurdity of the
old practice was noticed in the prologue written for
this revival of *Othello*, which was made memorable
by the innovation. Some lines in the prologue
describe the earlier system thus:—

> For to speak truth, men act, that are between
> Forty or fifty, wenches of fifteen,
> With bone so large and nerve so uncompliant,
> When you call Desdemona, enter Giant.

Profound commiseration seems due to the
Elizabethan playgoer, who was liable to have his
faith in the tenderness and gentleness of Desdemona rudely shaken by the irruption on the stage of
a brawny, broad-shouldered athlete, masquerading
in her sweet name. Boys or men of all shapes and
sizes squeaking or bawling out the tender and
pathetic lines of Shakespeare's heroines, and no
joys of scenery to distract the playgoer from the uncouth inconsistency! At first sight it would seem
that the Elizabethan playgoer's lot was anything
but happy.

VII

The Elizabethan's hard fate strangely contrasts
with the situation of the playgoer of the nineteenth
or twentieth century. To the latter Shakespeare is

presented in a dazzling plenitude of colour.   Music
punctuates not merely intervals between scenes and
acts, but critical pauses in the speeches of the
actors.   Pictorial tableaux enthral the most callous
onlooker.   Very striking is the contrast offered by
the methods of representation accepted with enthusiasm by the Elizabethan playgoer and those
deemed essential by the fashionable modern manager.   There seems a relish of barbarism in the
ancient system when it is compared with the one
now in vogue.

I fear the final conclusion to be drawn from the
contrast is, contrary to expectation, more credit-
able to our ancestors than to ourselves.   The
needful dramatic illusion was obviously evoked in
the playgoer of the past with an ease that is unknown to the present patrons of the stage.   The
absence of scenery, the substitution of boys and men
for women, could only have passed muster with
the Elizabethan spectator because he was able to
realise the dramatic potency of the poet's work
without any, or any but the slightest, adventitious
aid outside the words of the play.

The Elizabethan playgoer needs no pity.   It is
ourselves who are deserving objects of compassion,
because we lack those qualities, the possession of
which enabled the Elizabethan to acknowledge in
Shakespeare's work, despite its manner of production, "the delight and wonder of his stage."   The
imaginative faculty was far from universal among
the Elizabethan playgoers.   The playgoing mob
always includes groundlings who delight exclusively in dumb shows and noise.   Many of Shakespeare's contemporaries complained that there were

playgoers who approved nothing "but puppetry and loved ridiculous antics," and that there were *entertain* men who, going to the playhouse only "to laugh and feed fool-fat," "checked at all goodness there."[1] No public of any age or country is altogether free from such infirmities. But the reception accorded to Shakespeare's plays in the theatre of his day, in contemporary theatrical conditions, is proof positive of a signal imaginative faculty in an exceptionally large proportion of the playgoers.

To the Elizabethan actor a warm tribute is due. Shakespeare has declared with emphasis that no amount of scenery can secure genuine success on the stage for a great work of the imagination. He is no less emphatic in the value he sets on competent acting. In *Hamlet,* as every reader will remember, the dramatist points out the perennial defects of the actor, and shows how they may and must be corrected. He did all he could for the Elizabethan playgoer in the way of insisting that the art of acting must be studied seriously and that the dramatist's words must reach the ears of the audience, clearly and intelligibly enunciated.

"Speak the speech, I pray you," he tells the actor, "as I pronounce it to you, trippingly on the tongue; but if you mouth it, as many of your players do, I had as lief the town-crier spoke my lines. Nor do not saw the air too much with your hand, thus; but use all gently: for in the very torrent, tempest, and—as I may say—whirlwind of passion, you must acquire and beget a temperance, that may give it smoothness.

"Be not too tame neither, but let your own

---

[1] Chapman's *Revenge of Bussy D'Ambois,* Act I., Sc. i.

discretion be your tutor: suit the action to the word, the word to the action; with this special observance, that you o'erstep not the modesty of nature. O! there be players, that I have seen play, and heard others praise, and that highly, not to speak it profanely, that, neither having the accent of Christians nor the gait of Christian, pagan, nor man, have so strutted and bellowed that I have thought some of nature's journeymen had made men and not made them well, they imitated humanity so abominably."

The player amiably responds: "I hope we have reformed that indifferently with us." Shakespeare in the person of Hamlet retorts in a tone of some impatience: "O! reform it altogether. And let those that play your clowns speak no more than is set down for them." The applause which welcomed Shakespeare's masterpieces on their first representation is adequate evidence that the leading Elizabethan actors in the main obeyed these instructions.

VIII

Nevertheless the final success of a great imaginative play on the stage does not depend entirely on the competence of the actor. Encircling and determining all conditions is the fitness of the audience. A great imaginative play well acted will not achieve genuine success unless the audience has at command sufficient imaginative power to induce in them an active sympathy with the efforts, not only of the actor, but of the dramatist.

It is not merely in the first chorus to *Henry V.* that Shakespeare has declared his conviction that the creation of the needful dramatic illusion is finally due to exercise of the imagination on the part of the audience.[1] Theseus, in *A Midsummer Night's Dream*, in the capacity of a spectator of a play which is rendered by indifferent actors, makes a somewhat depreciatory reflection on the character of acting, whatever its degree or capacity. But the value of Theseus's deliverance lies in its clear definition of the part which the audience has to play, if it do its duty by great drama.

"The best in this kind," says Theseus of actors, "are but shadows, and the worst are no worse, *if imagination amend them*." To which Hippolyta, less tolerant than Theseus of the incapacity of the players to whom she is listening, tartly retorts: "It must be your imagination (*i.e.*, the spectator's), then, and not theirs" (*i.e.*, the actors').

These sentences mean that at its very best acting is but a shadow or simulation of life, and that acting at its very worst is likewise a shadow or simulation. But the imagination of the audience is supreme controller of the theatre, and can, if it be of adequate intensity, even cause inferior acting to yield effects hardly distinguishable from those of the best.

It would be unwise to press Theseus's words to extreme limits. All that it behoves us to deduce from them is the unimpeachable principle that the success of the romantic drama on the stage depends not merely on the actors' gift of imagination, but to an even larger extent on the possession by the audience of a similar faculty. Good acting is needful. Scenery in moderation will aid the dramatic

[1] See pages 20–21 *supra*.

illusion, although excess of scenery or scenic machinery may destroy it altogether. Dramatic illusion must ultimately spring from the active and unrestricted exercise of the imaginative faculty by author, actor, and audience in joint-partnership.

What is the moral to be deduced from any examination of the Elizabethan playgoer's attitude to Shakespeare's plays? It is something of this kind. We must emulate our ancestors' command of the imagination. We must seek to enlarge our imaginative sympathy with Shakespeare's poetry. The imaginative faculty will not come to us at our call; it will not come to us by the mechanism of study; it may not come to us at all. It is easier to point out the things that will hinder than the things that will hasten its approach. Absorption in the material needs of life, the concentration of energy on the increase of worldly goods, leave little room for the entrance into the brain of the imaginative faculty, or for its free play when it is there. The best way of seeking it is by reading the greatest of great imaginative literature, by freely yielding the mind to its influence, and by exercising the mind under its sway. And the greatest imaginative literature that was ever penned was penned by Shakespeare. No counsel is wiser than that of those two personal friends of his, who were the first editors of his work and penned words to this effect: "Read him therefore, and again and again, and then if you do not like him, surely you are in some manifest danger" of losing a saving grace of life.

III

SHAKESPEARE IN ORAL TRADITION [1]

I

BIOGRAPHERS did not lie in wait for men of eminence
on their death-beds in Shakespeare's epoch. To the
advantage of literature, and to the less than might
be anticipated disadvantage of history (for your
death-bed biographer, writing under kinsfolk's tear-
laden eyes, must needs be smoother-tongued than
truthful), the place of the modern memoir-writer
was filled in Shakespeare's day by friendly poets,
who were usually alert to pay fit homage in elegiac
verse to a dead hero's achievements. In that regard, Shakespeare's poetic friends showed at his
death exceptional energy. During his lifetime men
of letters had bestowed on his "reigning wit," on
his kingly supremacy of genius, most generous stores
of eulogy. Within two years of the end a son-
neteer had justly deplored that something of Shakespeare's own power, to which he deprecated pre-
tension, was needful to those who should praise him
aright. But when Shakespeare lay dead in the
spring of 1616, when, as one of his admirers topically
phrased it, he had withdrawn from the stage of the

---

[1] This paper was first printed in *The Nineteenth Century and
After*, February, 1902.

world to the "tiring-house" or dressing-room of the grave, the flood of panegyrical lamentation was not checked by the sense of literary inferiority which in all sincerity oppressed the spirits of surviving companions.

One of the earliest of the elegies was a sonnet by William Basse, who gave picturesque expression to the conviction that Shakespeare would enjoy for all time an unique reverence on the part of his countrymen. In the opening lines of his poem Basse apostrophised Chaucer, Spenser, and the dramatist Francis Beaumont, three poets who had already received the recognition of burial in Westminster Abbey—Beaumont, the youngest of them, only five weeks before Shakespeare died. To this honoured trio Basse made appeal to "lie a thought more nigh" one another, so as to make room for the newly-dead Shakespeare within their "sacred sepulchre." Then, in the second half of his sonnet, the poet, developing a new thought, argued that Shakespeare, in right of his pre-eminence, merited a burial-place apart from all his fellows. With a glance at Shakespeare's distant grave in the chancel of Stratford-on-Avon Church, the writer exclaimed:

> Under this carved marble of thine own
> Sleep, brave tragedian, Shakespeare, sleep *alone.*

The fine sentiment found many a splendid echo. It resounded in Ben Jonson's lines of 1623:—

> My Shakespeare, rise! I will not lodge thee by
> Chaucer, or Spenser, or bid Beaumont lie
> A little further to make thee a room.
> Thou art a monument without a tomb,
> And art alive still, while thy book doth live
> And we have wits to read and praise to give.

Milton wrote a few years later, in 1630, how Shakespeare, "sepulchred" in "the monument" of his writings,

in such pomp doth lie,
That kings for such a tomb would wish to die.

Never was a glorious immortality foretold for any man with more solemn confidence than it was foretold for Shakespeare at his death by his circle of adorers. When Time, one elegist said, should dissolve his "Stratford monument," the laurel about Shakespeare's brow would wear its greenest hue. Shakespeare's critical friend, Ben Jonson, was but one of a numerous band who imagined the "sweet swan of Avon," "the star of poets," shining for ever as a constellation in the firmament. Such was the invariable temper in which literary men gave vent to their grief on learning the death of the "beloved author," "the famous scenicke poet," "the admirable dramaticke poet," "that famous writer and actor," "worthy master William Shakespeare" of Stratford-on-Avon.

II

Unqualified and sincere was the eulogy awarded to Shakespeare, alike in his lifetime and immediately after his death. But the spirit and custom of the age confided to future generations the duty of first offering him the more formal honour of prosaic and critical biography. The biographic memoir, which consists of precise and duly authenticated dates and records of domestic and professional experiences and achievements, was in England a comparatively late growth. It had no existence when Shakespeare died. It began to blossom in the eighteenth century, and did not flourish luxuriantly till a far more recent period. Meagre seeds of the modern art of biography were, indeed, sown within a few years of Shakespeare's death; but outside the unique little field of Izaak Walton's tillage, the first sproutings were plants so different from the fully developed tree, that they can with difficulty be identified with the genus. Apart from Izaak Walton's exceptional efforts, the biographical spirit first betrayed itself in England in slender, occasional pamphlets of rhapsodical froth, after the model of the funeral sermon. There quickly followed more substantial volumes of collective biography which mainly supplied arbitrarily compiled, if extended, catalogues of names. To each name were attached brief annotations, which occasionally offered a fact or a date, but commonly consisted of a few sentences of grotesque, uncritical eulogy.

Fuller's *Worthies of England*, which was begun about 1643 and was published posthumously in 1662, was the first English compendium of biography of this aboriginal pattern. Shakespeare naturally found place in Fuller's merry pages, for the author loved in his eccentric fashion his country's literature, and he had sought the society of those who had come to close quarters with literary heroes of the past generation. Of that generation his own life just touched the fringe, he being eight years old when Shakespeare died. Fuller described the dramatist as a native of Stratford-on-Avon, who "was in some sort a compound of three eminent poets"—Martial, "in the warlike sound of his name"; Ovid, for the naturalness and wit of his poetry; and Plautus, alike for the extent of his comic power and his lack of scholarly training.   He was, Fuller continued, an eminent instance of the rule that a poet is born not made.   "Though his genius," he warns us, "generally was jocular and inclining him to festivity, yet he could, when so disposed, be solemn and serious."   His comedies, Fuller adds, would rouse laughter even in the weeping philosopher Heraclitus, while his tragedies would bring tears even to the eyes of the laughing philosopher Democritus.

Of positive statements respecting Shakespeare's career Fuller is economical.   He commits himself to nothing more than may be gleaned from the following sentences:—

Many were the wit-combats betwixt him and Ben Jonson; which two I behold like a Spanish great galleon and an English man-of-war; master Jonson (like the former) was built far higher in learning; solid, but slow, in his performances.   Shakespeare, with the English man-of-war, lesser in bulk, but lighter in sailing, could turn with all tides, tack about, and take advantage of all winds, by the quickness of his wit and invention.   He died *Anno Domini* 1616, and was buried at Stratford-upon-Avon, the town of his nativity.

Fuller's successors did their work better in some regards, because they laboured in narrower fields. Many of them showed a welcome appreciation of a main source of their country's permanent reputation by confining their energies to the production of biographical catalogues, not of all manners of heroes, but solely of those who had distinguished

themselves in poetry and the drama.[1]   In 1675 a
biographical catalogue of poets was issued for the
first time in England, and the example once set was
quickly followed. No less than three more efforts
of the like kind came to fruition before the end of
the century.

In all four biographical manuals Shakespeare
was accorded more or less imposing space. Although
Fuller's eccentric compliments were usually repeated, they were mingled with far more extended
and discriminating tributes. Two of the com-
pilers designated Shakespeare "the glory of the
English stage"; a third wrote, "I esteem his plays
beyond any that have ever been published in our
language"; while the fourth quoted with approval
Dryden's fine phrase: "Shakespeare was the Man
who of all Modern and perhaps Ancient Poets had
the largest and most comprehensive Soul." But
the avowed principles of these tantalising volumes
justify no expectation of finding in them solid information. The biographical cataloguers of the
seventeenth century did little more than proclaim
Shakespeare and the other great poets of the country
to be fit subjects for formal biography as soon as
the type should be matured. That was the message
of greatest virtue which these halting chroniclers
delivered.

In Shakespeare's case their message was not
long neglected. In 1709 Nicholas Rowe, after-

[1] Such a compilation had been contemplated in 1614, two
years before the dramatist died, by one of Shakespeare's own
associates, Thomas Heywood. Twenty-one years later, in 1635,
Heywood spoke of " committing to the public view " his sum-
mary *Lives of the Poets*, but nothing more was heard of that
project.

wards George the First's poet laureate, published
the first professed biography of the poet. The
eminence of the subject justified such alacrity, and
it had no precise parallel. More or less definite
lives of a few of Shakespeare's great literary contemporaries followed his biography at long intervals.
But the whole field has never been occupied by the
professed biographer. In some cases the delay has
meant loss of opportunity for ever. Very many
distinguished Elizabethan and Jacobean authors
have shared the fate of John Webster, next to
Shakespeare the most eminent tragic dramatist of
the era, of whom no biography was ever attempted,
and no positive biographic fact survives.

But this is an imperfect statement of the advantages which Shakespeare's career enjoyed above that
of his fellows from the commemorative point of
view. Although formal biography did not lay
hand on his name for nearly a century after his
death, the authentic tradition of his life and work
began steadily to crystallise in the minds and mouths
of men almost as soon as he drew his last breath.
Fuller's characteristically shadowy hint of "wit-
combats betwixt Shakespeare and Ben Jonson"
and of the contrasted characters of the two com-
batants, suggests pretty convincingly that Shakespeare's name presented to the seventeenth-century
imagination and tongue a better defined personality
and experience than the embryonic biographer knew
how to disclose. The commemorative instinct never
seeks satisfaction in biographic effort exclusively,
even when the art of biography has ripened into
satisfying fulness. A great man's reputation and
the moving incidents of his career never live solely

in the printed book or the literary word.   In a great
man's life-time, and for many years after, his fame
and his fortunes live most effectually on living lips.
The talk of surviving kinsmen, fellow-craftsmen,
admiring acquaintances, and sympathetic friends is'
the treasure-house which best preserves the personality of the dead hero for those who come soon
after him.   When biography is unpractised, no
other treasure-house is available.

The report of such converse moves quickly from
mouth to mouth.   In its progress the narration
naturally grows fainter, and, when no biographer
lies in wait for it, ultimately perishes altogether.
But oral tradition respecting a great man whose
work has fascinated the imagination of his countrymen comes into circulation early, persists long,
even in the absence of biography, and safeguards
substantial elements of truth through many generations.   Although no biographer put in an appearance, it is seldom that some fragment of oral tradition respecting a departed hero is not committed
to paper by one or other amateur gossip who comes
within earshot of it early in its career.   The casual
unsifted record of floating anecdote is not always
above suspicion.   As a rule it is embodied in familiar
correspondence, or in diaries, or in commonplace
books, where clear and definite language is rarely
met with; but, however disappointingly imperfect
and trivial, however disjointed, however deficient
in literary form the registered jottings of oral tradition may be, it is in them, if they exist at all with
any title to credit, that future ages best realise the
fact that the great man was in plain truth a living
entity, and no mere shadow of a name.

III

When Shakespeare died, on the 23rd of April, 1616, many men and women were alive who had come into personal association with him, and there were many more who had heard of him from those who had spoken with him. Apart from his numerous kinsfolk and neighbours at Stratford-on-Avon, there was in London a large society of fellow-authors and fellow-actors with whom he lived in close communion. Very little correspondence or other intimate memorials, whether of Shakespeare's professional friends or of his kinsfolk or country neighbours, survive. Nevertheless some scraps of the talk about Shakespeare that circulated among his acquaintances or was handed on by them to the next generation has been tracked to written paper of the seventeenth century and to printed books. A portion of these scattered memorabilia of the earliest known oral traditions respecting Shakespeare has come to light very recently; other portions have been long accessible. As a connected whole they have never been narrowly scrutinised, and I believe it may serve a useful purpose to consider with some minuteness how the mass of them came into being, and what is the sum of information they conserve.

The more closely Shakespeare's career is studied the plainer it becomes that his experiences and fortunes were identical with those of all who followed in his day his profession of dramatist, and that his conscious aims and ambitions and practices were those of every contemporary man of letters. The difference between the results of his endeavours and those of his fellows was due to the magic and in-

voluntary working of genius, which, since the birth
of poetry, has exercised "as large a charter as the
wind, to blow on whom it pleases." Speculation
or debate as to why genius bestowed its fullest inspiration on Shakespeare is no less futile than
speculation or debate as to why he was born into
the world with a head on his shoulders instead of a
block of stone. It is enough for wise men to know
the obvious fact that genius endowed Shakespeare
with its richest gifts, and a very small acquaintance
with the literary history of the world and with the
manner, in which genius habitually plays its part
there, will show the folly of cherishing astonishment that Shakespeare, rather than one more nobly
born or more academically trained, should have
been chosen for the glorious dignity. Nowhere is
this lesson more convincingly taught than by a systematic survey of the oral tradition. Shakespeare
figures there as a supremely favoured heir of genius,
whose humility of birth and education merely serves
to intensify the respect due to his achievement.

In London, where Shakespeare's work was mainly
done and his fortune and reputation achieved, he
lived with none in more intimate social relations
than with the leading members of his own prosperous company of actors, which, under the patronage
of the king, produced his greatest plays. Like himself, most of his colleagues were men of substance,
sharers with him in the two most fashionable theatres
of the metropolis, occupiers of residences in both
town and country, owners of houses and lands, and
bearers of coat-armour of that questionable validity
which commonly attaches to the heraldry of the
nouveaux riches. Two of these affluent associates

predeceased Shakespeare; and one of them, Augustine Phillips, attested his friendship in a small legacy. Three of Shakespeare's fellow-actors were affectionately remembered by him in his will, and a fourth, one of the youngest members of the company, proved his regard for Shakespeare's memory by taking, a generation after the dramatist's death, Charles Hart, Shakespeare's grand-nephew, into his employ as a "boy" or apprentice. Grand-nephew Charles went forth on a prosperous career, in which at its height he was seriously likened to his grand-uncle's most distinguished actor-ally, Richard Burbage. Above all is it to be borne in mind that to the disinterested admiration for his genius of two fellow-members of Shakespeare's company we owe the preservation and publication of the greater part of his literary work. The personal fascination of "so worthy a friend and fellow as was our Shakespeare" bred in all his fellow-workers an affectionate pride in their intimacy.

Such men were the parents of the greater part of the surviving oral tradition of Shakespeare, and no better parentage could be wished for. To the first accessible traditions of proved oral currency after Shakespeare's death, the two fellow-actors who called the great First Folio into existence pledged their credit in writing only seven years after his death. They printed in the preliminary pages of that volume these three statements of common fame, viz., that to Shakespeare and his plays in his lifetime was invariably extended the fullest favour of the court and its leading officers; that death deprived him of the opportunity he had long contemplated of preparing his literary work for the press; and that he wrote with so rapidly flowing a pen that his manuscript was never defaced by alteration or erasure. Shakespeare's extraordinary rapidity of composition was an especially frequent topic of contemporary debate. Ben Jonson, the most intimate personal friend of Shakespeare outside the circle of working actors, wrote how "the players" would "often mention" to him the poet's fluency, and how he was in the habit of arguing that Shakespeare's work would have been the better had he devoted more time to its correction. The players, Ben Jonson adds, were wont to grumble that such a remark was "malevolent," and he delighted in seeking to vindicate it to them on what seemed to him to be just critical grounds.

The copious deliverances of Jonson in the tavern-parliaments of the London wits, which were in almost continuous session during the first four decades of the seventeenth century, set flowing much other oral tradition of Shakespeare, whom Jonson said he loved and whose memory he honoured "on this side idolatry as much as any." One of Jonson's remarks which seems to have lived longest on the lips of contemporaries was that Shakespeare "was indeed honest and [like his own Othello] of an open and free nature,[1] had an excellent phantasy, brave notions and gentle expressions, wherein he flowed with that facility that sometimes it was necessary he should be stopped."

To the same category of oral tradition belongs the further piece which Fuller enshrined in his slender biography with regard to Shakespeare's

---

[1] Iago says of Othello, in *Othello*, I., iii., 405: "The Moor is *of a free and open nature.*"

alert skirmishes with Ben Jonson in dialectical
battle. Jonson's dialectical skill was for a long
period undisputed, and for gossip to credit Shakespeare with victory in such conflict was to pay his
memory even more enviable honour than Jonson
paid it in his own *obiter dicta*.

There is yet an additional scrap of oral tradition
which, reduced to writing about the time that
Fuller was at work, confirms Shakespeare's reputation for quickness of wit in everyday life, especially
in intercourse with the critical giant Jonson. Dr.
Donne, the Jacobean poet and dean of St. Paul's,
told, apparently on Jonson's authority, the story
that Shakespeare, having consented to act as godfather to one of Jonson's sons, solemnly promised
to give the child a dozen good "*Latin* spoons" for
the father to "translate." *Latin* was a play upon
the word "latten," which was the name of a metal
resembling brass. The simple quip was a good-
humoured hit at Jonson's pride in his classical learning. Dr. Donne related the anecdote to Sir Nicholas
L'Estrange, a country gentleman of literary tastes,
who had no interest in Shakespeare except from
the literary point of view. He entered it in his
commonplace book within thirty years of Shakespeare's death.

IV

Of the twenty-five actors who are enumerated in
a preliminary page of the great First Folio, as filling
in Shakespeare's lifetime chief *rôles* in his plays, few
survived him long. All of them came in personal
contact with him; several of them constantly appeared with him on the stage from early days.

The two who were longest lived, John Lowin and

Joseph Taylor, came at length to bear a great weight of years. They were both Shakespeare's juniors, Lowin by twelve years, and Taylor by twenty, but both established their reputation before middle age. Lowin at twenty-seven took part with Shakespeare in the first representation of Ben Jonson's *Sejanus* in 1603. He was an early, if not the first, interpreter of the character of Falstaff. Taylor as understudy to the great actor Burbage, a very close ally of Shakespeare, seems to have achieved some success in the part of Hamlet, and to have been applauded in the rôle of Iago, while the dramatist yet lived. When the dramatist died, Lowin was forty, and Taylor over thirty.

Subsequently, as their senior colleagues one by one passed from the world, these two actors assumed first rank in their company, and before the ruin in which the Civil War involved all theatrical enterprise, they were acknowledged to stand at the head of their profession.[1] Taylor lived through the Commonwealth, and Lowin far into the reign of Charles the Second, ultimately reaching his ninety-third year. Their last days were passed in indigence, and Lowin when an octogenarian was reduced to keeping the inn of the "Three Pigeons," at Brentford.

Both these men kept alive from personal knowledge some oral Shakespearean tradition during the

[1] Like almost all their colleagues, they had much literary taste. When public events compulsorily retired them from the stage, they, with the aid of the dramatist Shirley and eight other actors, two of whom were members with them of Shakespeare's old company, did an important service to English literature. In 1647 they collected for first publication in folio Beaumont and Fletcher's plays; only one, *The Wild Goose Chase*, was omitted, and that piece Taylor and Lowin brought out by their unaided efforts five years later.

fifty years and more that followed his death.   Little
of their gossip is extant.   But some of it was put
on record, before the end of the century, by John
Downes, the old prompter and librarian of a chief
London theatre.   According to Downes's testimony,
Taylor repeated instructions which he had received from Shakespeare's own lips for the playing
of the part of Hamlet, while Lowin narrated how
Shakespeare taught him the theatrical interpretation of the character of Henry the Eighth, in that
play of the name which came from the joint pens
of Shakespeare and Fletcher.

Both Taylor's and Lowin's reminiscences were
passed on to Thomas Betterton, the greatest actor
of the Restoration, and the most influential figure
in the theatrical life of his day.   Through him they
were permanently incorporated in the verbal stage-
lore of the country.   No doubt is possible of the
validity of this piece of oral tradition, which re-
veals Shakespeare in the act of personally supervis-
ing the production of his own plays, and springs
from the mouths of those who personally benefited
by the dramatist's activity.

Taylor and Lowin were probably the last actors
to speak of Shakespeare from personal knowledge.
But hardly less deserving of attention are scraps of
gossip about Shakespeare which survive in writing,
on the authority of some of Taylor's and Lowin's
actor-contemporaries.   These men were never themselves in personal relations with Shakespeare, but
knew many formerly in direct relation with him.
Probably the seventeenth century actor with the
most richly stored memory of the oral Shakespearean tradition was William Beeston, to whose

house in Hog Lane, Shoreditch, the curious often resorted in Charles the Second's time to listen to his reminiscences of Shakespeare and of the poets of Shakespeare's epoch.

Beeston died after a busy theatrical life, at eighty or upwards, in 1682. He belonged to a family of distinguished actors or actor-managers. His father, brothers, and son were all, like himself, prominent in the profession, and some of them were almost as long-lived as himself. His own career combined with that of his father covered more than a century, and both sedulously and with pride cultivated intimacy with contemporary dramatic authors.

It was probably William Beeston's grandfather, also William Beeston, to whom the satirical Elizabethan, Thomas Nash, dedicated in 1593, with good-humoured irony, one of his insolent libels on Gabriel Harvey, a scholar who had defamed the memory of a dead friend. Nash laughed at his patron's struggles with syntax in his efforts to write poetry, and at his indulgence in drink, which betrayed itself in his red nose. But, in spite of Nash's characteristic frankness, he greeted the first William Beeston as a boon companion who was generous in his entertainment of threadbare scholars. Christopher Beeston, this man's son, the father of the Shakespearean gossip, had in abundance the hereditary taste for letters. He was at one time Shakespeare's associate on the stage. Both took part together in the first representation of Ben Jonson's *Every Man in His Humour*, in 1598. His name was again linked with Shakespeare's in the will of their fellow-actor, Augustine Phillips, who left each of them a legacy as a token of friendship at his death in 1605. Christopher Beeston left Shakespeare's company of

actors for another theatre early in his career, and his
closest friend among the actor-authors of his day in
later life was not Shakespeare himself but Thomas
Heywood, the popular dramatist and pamphleteer,
who lived on to 1650. This was a friendship which
kept Beeston's respect for Shakespeare at a fitting
pitch. Heywood, who wrote the affectionate lines:

> Mellifluous Shakespeare, whose inchanting Quill
> Commanded Mirth or Passion, was but *Will*,

enjoys the distinction of having published in Shakespeare's lifetime the only expression of resentment
that is known to have come from the dramatist's
proverbially "gentle lips." Shakespeare (Heywood
wrote) "was much offended" with an unprincipled
publisher who "presumed to make so bold with his
name" as to put it to a book of which he was not
the author. And Beeston had direct concern with
the volume called *An Apology for Actors*, to which
Heywood appended his report of these words of
Shakespeare. To the book the actor Beeston contributed preliminary verses addressed to the author,
his "good friend and fellow, Thomas Heywood."
There Beeston briefly vindicated the recreation
which the playhouse offered the public. Much
else in Christopher Beeston's professional career is
known, but it is sufficient to mention here that he
died in 1637, while he was filling the post that he
had long held, of manager to the King and Queen's
Company of Players at Cock-pit Theatre in Drury
Lane. It was the chief playhouse of the time, and
his wife was lessee of it.

Christopher's son, William Beeston the second,
was his father's coadjutor at Drury Lane, and
succeeded him in his high managerial office there.
The son encountered difficulties with the Govern-

ment through an alleged insult to the King in one
of the pieces that he produced, and he had to retire
from the Cock-pit to a smaller theatre in Salisbury
Court. Until his death he retained the respect of
the play-going and the literature-loving public, and
his son George, whom he brought up to the stage,
carried on the family repute to a later generation.

William Beeston had no liking for dissolute
society, and the open vice of Charles the Second's
Court pained him. He lived in old age much in
seclusion, but by a congenial circle he was always
warmly welcomed for the freshness and enthusiasm
of his talk about the poets who flourished in his
youth. "Divers times (in my hearing)," one of his
auditors, Francis Kirkman, an ardent collector,
reader, and publisher of old plays, wrote to him in
1652—"Divers times (in my hearing), to the admiration of the whole company you have most
judiciously discoursed of Poesie." In the judgment of Kirkman, his friend, the old actor, was
"the happiest interpreter and judg of our English
stage-Playes this Nation ever produced; which the
Poets and Actors these times cannot (without in-
gratitude) deny; for I have heard the chief, and
most ingenious of them, acknowledg their Fames
and Profits essentially sprung from your instructions, judgment, and fancy." Few who heard
Beeston talk failed, Kirkman continues, to sub-
scribe "to his opinion that no Nation could glory
in such Playes" as those that came from the pens
of the great Elizabethans, Shakespeare, Fletcher,
and Ben Jonson. "Glorious John Dryden" shared
in the general enthusiasm for the veteran Beeston,
and bestowed on him the title of "the chronicle of

the stage"; while John Aubrey, the honest antiquary and gossip, who had in his disorderly brain the makings of a Boswell, sought Beeston's personal acquaintance about 1660, in order to "take from him the lives of the old English Poets."

It is Aubrey who has recorded most of such sparse fragments of Beeston's talk as survive—how Edmund "Spenser was a little man, wore short hair, little bands, and short cuffs," and how Sir John Suckling came to invent the game of cribbage. Naturally, of Shakespeare Beeston has much to relate. In the shrewd old gossip's language, he "did act exceedingly well," far better than Jonson; "he understood Latin pretty well, for he had been in his younger years a schoolmaster in the country"; "he was a handsome, well-shaped man, very good company, and of a very ready and pleasant smooth wit"; he and Ben Jonson gathered "humours of men daily wherever they came." The ample testimony to the excellent influence which Beeston exercised over "the poets and actors of these times" leaves little doubt that Sir William D'Avenant, Beeston's successor as manager at Drury Lane, and Thomas Shadwell, the fashionable writer of comedies, largely echoed their old mentor's words when, in conversation with Aubrey, they credited Shakespeare with "a most prodigious wit," and declared that they "did admire his natural parts beyond all other dramatical writers." [1]

John Lacy, another actor of Beeston's generation, who made an immense reputation on the stage

[1] Aubrey's *Lives*, being reports of his miscellaneous gossip, were first fully printed from his manuscripts in the Bodleian Library by the Clarendon Press in 1898. They were most carefully edited by the Rev. Andrew Clark.

and was also a successful writer of farces, was one of Beeston's closest friends, and, having been personally acquainted with Ben Jonson, could lend to many of Beeston's stories useful corroborative testimony. With Lacy, too, the gossip Aubrey conversed of Shakespeare's career.

At the same time, the popularity of Shakespeare's grand-nephew, Charles Hart, who was called the Burbage of his day, whetted among' actors the appetite for Shakespearean tradition, especially of the theatrical kind. Hart had no direct acquaintance with his great kinsman, who died fully ten years before he was born, while his father, who was sixteen at Shakespeare's death, died in his son's boyhood. But Hart's grandmother, the poet's sister, lived till he was twenty-one, and Richard Robinson, the fellow-member of Shakespeare's company who first taught Hart to act, survived his pupil's adolescence. That Hart did what he could to satisfy the curiosity of his companions there is a precise oral tradition to confirm. According to the story, first put on record in the eighteenth century by the painstaking antiquary, William Oldys, it was through Hart that some actors made, near the date of the Restoration, the exciting discovery that Gilbert, one of Shakespeare's brothers, who was the dramatist's junior by only two years, was still living at a patriarchal age. Oldys describes the concern with which Hart's professional acquaintances questioned the old man about his brother, and their disappointment when his failing memory only enabled him to recall William's performance of the part of Adam in his comedy of *As You Like It*.

It should be added that Oldys obtained his
information of the episode, which deserves more
attention than it has received, from an actor of a
comparatively recent generation, John Bowman,
who died over eighty in 1739, after spending "more
than half an age on the London theatres."

V

Valuable as these actors' testimonies are, it is in
another rank of the profession that we find the most
important link in the chain of witnesses alike to the
persistence and authenticity of the oral tradition of
Shakespeare which was current in the middle of the
seventeenth century. Sir William D'Avenant, the
chief playwright and promoter of theatrical enterprise of his day, enjoyed among persons of influence
and quality infinite credit and confidence. As a boy
he and his brothers had come into personal relations with the dramatist under their father's roof,
and the experience remained the proudest boast of
their lives. D'Avenant was little more than ten
when Shakespeare died, and his direct intercourse
with him was consequently slender; but D'Avenant
was a child of the Muses, and his slight acquaintance
with the living Shakespeare spurred him to treasure
all that he could learn of his hero from any who
had enjoyed fuller opportunities of intimacy.

To learn the manner in which the child
D'Avenant and his brothers came to know Shakespeare is to approach the dramatist through oral
tradition at very close quarters. D'Avenant's father, a melancholy person who was never known
to laugh, long kept at Oxford the Crown Inn in Car-
fax. Gossip which was current in Oxford through-

out the seventeenth century, and was put on record before the end of it by more than one scholar of the university, establishes the fact that Shakespeare on his annual journeys between London and Stratford-on-Avon was in the habit of staying at the elder D'Avenant's Oxford hostelry. The report ran that "he was exceedingly respected" in the house, and was freely admitted to the inn-keeper's domestic circle. The inn-keeper's wife was credited with a mercurial disposition which contrasted strangely with her husband's sardonic temperament; it was often said in Oxford that Shakespeare not merely found his chief attraction at the Crown Inn in the wife's witty conversation, but formed a closer intimacy with her than moralists would approve. Oral tradition speaks in clearer tones of his delight in the children of the family—four boys and three girls. We have at command statements on that subject from the lips of two of the sons. The eldest son, Robert, who was afterwards a parson in Wiltshire, and was on familiar terms with many men of culture, often recalled with pride for their benefit that "Mr William Shakespeare" had given him as a child "a hundred kisses" in his father's tavern-parlour.

The third son, William, was more expansive in his reminiscences. It was generally understood at Oxford in the early years of the seventeenth century that he was the poet's godson, as his Christian name would allow, but some gossips had it that the poet's paternity was of a less spiritual character. According to a genuine anecdote of contemporary origin, when the boy, William D'Avenant, in Shakespeare's lifetime, informed a doctor of the university that he was on his way to ask a blessing of his godfather who had just arrived in the town, the child was warned by his interlocutor against taking the name of God in vain. It is proof of the estimation in which D'Avenant held Shakespeare that when he came to man's estate he was "content enough to have" the insinuation "thought to be true." He would talk freely with his friends over a glass of wine of Shakespeare's visits to his father's house, and would say "that it seemed to him that he wrote with Shakespeare's very spirit." Of his reverence for Shakespeare he gave less questionable proof in a youthful elegy in which he represented the flowers and trees on the banks of the Avon mourning for Shakespeare's death and the river weeping itself away. He was credited, too, with having adopted the new spelling of his name D'*Aven*ant (for Davenant), so as to read into it a reference to the river Avon.

In maturer age D'Avenant sought out the old actors Taylor and Lowin, and mastered their information respecting Shakespeare, their early colleague on the stage. With a curious perversity he mainly devoted his undoubted genius in his later years to rewriting in accordance with the debased taste of Charles the Second's reign the chief works of his idol; but until D'Avenant's death in 1668 the unique character of Shakespeare's greatness had no stouter champion than he, and in the circle of men of wit and fashion, of which he was the centre, none kept the cult alive with greater enthusiasm. His early friend Sir John Suckling, the Cavalier poet, who was only seven years old when Shakespeare died, he infected so thoroughly with his own affectionate admiration that Suckling wrote of the dramatist in familiar letters as "my friend Mr William Shakespeare," and had his portrait painted by Vandyck with an open volume of Shakespeare's works in his hand. Even more important is Dryden's testimony that he was himself "first taught" by D'Avenant "to admire" Shakespeare.

One of the most precise and valuable pieces of oral tradition which directly owed currency to D'Avenant was the detailed story of the generous gift of £1000, which Shakespeare's patron, the Earl of Southampton, made the poet "to enable him to go through with a purchase which he heard he had a mind to."   Rowe, Shakespeare's first biographer, recorded this particular on the specific authority of D'Avenant, who, he pointed out, "was probably very well acquainted with the dramatist's affairs."   At the same time it was often repeated that D'Avenant was owner of a complimentary letter which James the First had written to Shakespeare with his own hand. A literary politician, John Sheffield, Earl of Mulgrave and Duke of Buckinghamshire, who survived D'Avenant nearly half a century, said that he had examined the epistle while it was in D'Avenant's keeping. The publisher Lintot first printed the Duke's statement in the preface to a new edition of Shakespeare's Poems in 1709.

D'Avenant's devotion did much for Shakespeare's memory; but it stimulated others to do even more for the after-generations who wished to know the whole truth about Shakespeare's life. The great actor of the Restoration, Thomas Betterton, was D'Avenant's close associate in his last years. D'Avenant coached him in the parts both of Hamlet and of Henry the Eighth, in the light of the instruction which he had derived through the medium of Taylor and Lowin from Shakespeare's own lips. But more to the immediate purpose is it to note that D'Avenant's ardour as a seeker after knowledge of Shakespeare fired Betterton into making a pilgrimage to Stratford-on-Avon to glean oral traditions of the dramatist's life there. Many other of Shakespeare's admirers had previously made Stratford Church, where stood his tomb, a place of pilgrimage, and Aubrey had acknowledged in haphazard fashion the value of Stratford gossip. But it was Betterton's visit that laid the train for the systematic union of the oral traditions of London and Stratford respectively.

It was not until the London and Warwickshire streams of tradition mingled in equal strength that a regular biography of Shakespeare was possible. Betterton was the efficient cause of this conjunction. All that Stratford-on-Avon revealed to him he put at the disposal of Nicholas Rowe, who was the first to attempt a formal memoir. Of Betterton's assistance Rowe made generous acknowledgment in these terms:—

I must own a particular Obligation to him [*i.e.*, Betterton] for the most considerable part of the Passages relating to his [*i.e.*, Shakespeare's] Life, which I have here transmitted to the Publick; his veneration for the Memory of Shakespear having engag'd him to make a Journey into Warwickshire, on purpose to gather up what Remains he could of a Name for which he had so great a Value.

VI

The contemporary epitaph on Shakespeare's tomb in Stratford-on-Avon Church, which acclaimed

Shakespeare a writer of supreme genius, gave the
inhabitants of the little town no opportunity of
ignoring at any period the fact that the greatest
poet of his era had been their fellow-townsman.
Stratford was indeed openly identified with Shakespeare's career from the earliest possible day, and
Sir William Dugdale, the first topographer of Warwickshire, writing about 1650, noted that the place
was memorable for having given "birth and sepul-
ture to our late famous poet Will Shakespeare." But
the obscure little town produced in the years that
followed Shakespeare's death none who left behind
records of their experience, and such fragments of oral
tradition of Shakespeare at Stratford as are extant
survive accidentally, with one notable exception, in the
manuscript notes of visitors, who, like Betterton, were
drawn thither by a veneration acquired elsewhere.

The one notable exception is John Ward, a
seventeenth-century vicar of Stratford, who settled
there in 1662, at the age of thirty-three, forty-six
years after Shakespeare's death. Ward remained
at Stratford till his death in 1681. He is the only
resident of the century who wrote down any of the
local story. Ward was a man of good sentiment.
He judged that it became a vicar of Stratford to
know his Shakespeare well, and one of his private
reminders for his own conduct runs—"Remember to
peruse Shakespeare's plays, and bee much versed in
them, that I may not bee ignorant in that matter."

Ward was a voluminous diarist and a faithful
chronicler as far as he cared to go. Shakespeare's
last surviving daughter, Judith Quiney, was dying
when he arrived in Stratford; but sons of Shakespeare's sister, Mistress Joan Hart, were still living

in the poet's birthplace in Henley Street. Ward seems, too, to have known Lady Barnard, Shakespeare's only grandchild and last surviving descendant, who, although she only occasionally visited Stratford after her second marriage in 1649, and her removal to her husband's residence at Abington, near the town of Northampton, retained much property in her native place till her death in 1670. Ward reported from local conversation six important details, viz., that Shakespeare retired to Stratford in his elder days; that he wrote at the most active period of his life two plays a year; that he made so large an income from his dramas that " he spent at the rate of £1000 a year "; that he entertained his literary friends Drayton and Jonson at "a merry meeting" shortly before his death, and that he died of its effects.

Oxford, which was only thirty-six miles distant, supplied the majority of Stratford tourists, who, before Betterton, gathered oral tradition there. Aubrey, the Oxford gossip, roughly noted six local items other than those which are embodied in Ward's diary, or are to be gleaned from Beeston's reminiscences, viz., that Shakespeare had as a lad helped his father in his trade of butcher; that one of the poet's companions in boyhood, who died young, had almost as extraordinary a "natural wit"; that Shakespeare betrayed very early signs of poetic genius; that he paid annual visits to his native place when his career was at its height; that he loved at tavern meetings in the town to chaff John Combe, the richest of his fellow-townsmen, who was accused of usurious practices; and finally, that he died possessed of a substantial fortune.

Until the end of the century, visitors were shown round the church by an aged parish clerk, some of whose gossip about Shakespeare was recorded by one of them in 1693. The old man came thus to supply two further items of information: how Shakespeare ran away in youth, and how he sought service at a playhouse, "and by this meanes had an opportunity to be what he afterwards proved." A different visitor to Stratford next year recorded in an extant letter to a friend yet more scraps of oral tradition. These were to the effect that "the great Shakespear" dreaded the removal of his bones to the charnel-house attached to the church; that he caused his grave to be dug seventeen feet deep; and that he wrote the rude warning against disturbing his bones, which was inscribed on his gravestone, in order to meet the capacity of the "very ignorant sort of people" whose business it was to look after burials.

Betterton gained more precise particulars—the date of baptism and the like—from an examination of the parochial records; but the most valuable piece of oral tradition with which the great actor's research must be credited was the account of Shakespeare's deer-stealing escapade at Charlecote. Another tourist from Oxford privately and independently put that anecdote into writing at the same date, but Rowe, who first gave it to the world in his biography, relied exclusively on Betterton's authority. At a little later period inquiries made at Stratford by a second actor, Bowman, yielded a trifle more. Bowman came to know a very reputable resident at Bridgtown, a hamlet adjoining Stratford, Sir William Bishop, whose family was of old standing there. Sir William was born ten years after Shakespeare died, and lived close to Stratford till 1700. He told Bowman that a part of Falstaff's character was drawn from a fellow-townsman at Stratford against whom Shakespeare cherished a grudge owing to his obduracy in some business transaction. Bowman repeated the story to Oldys, who put it on record.

Although one could wish the early oral tradition of Stratford to have been more thoroughly reported, such as is extant in writing is sufficient to prove that Shakespeare's literary eminence was well known in his native place during the century that followed his death. In many villages in the neighbourhood of Stratford—at Bidford, at Wilmcote, at Greet, at Dursley—there long persisted like oral tradition of Shakespeare's occasional visits, but these were not written down before the middle of the eighteenth century; and although they are of service as proof of the local dissemination of his fame, they are some-what less definite than the traditions that suffered earlier record, and need not be particularised here. One light piece of gossip, which was associated with a country parish at some distance from Stratford, can alone be traced back to remote date, and was quickly committed to writing. A trustworthy Oxford don, Josias Howe, fellow and tutor of Trinity, was born early in the seventeenth century at Grendon in Buckinghamshire, where his father was long rector, and he maintained close relations with his birthplace during his life of more than ninety years. Grendon was on the road between Oxford and London. Howe stated that Shakespeare often visited the place in his journey from Stratford, and that he found the original of his character of Dog-

berry in the person of a parish constable who lived
on there till 1642. Howe was on familiar terms
with the man, and he confided his reminiscence to
his friend Aubrey, who duly recorded it, although
in a somewhat confused shape.

VII

It is with early oral tradition of Shakespeare's
personal experience that I am dealing here. It is
not my purpose to notice early literary criticism, of
which there is abundant supply. It was obviously
the free circulation of the fame of Shakespeare's
work which stimulated the activity of interest in his
private fortunes and led to the chronicling of the
oral tradition regarding them. It could easily be
shown that, outside the circle of professional poets,
dramatists, actors, and fellow-townsmen, Shakespeare's name was, from his first coming into public
notice, constantly on the lips of scholars, states-
men, and men of fashion who had any glimmer of
literary taste. The Muse of History indeed drops
plain hints of the views expressed at the social meetings of the great in the seventeenth century when
Shakespeare was under discussion. Before 1643,
" all persons of equality that had wit and learning"
engaged in a set debate at Eton in the rooms of
"the ever-memorable" John Hales, Fellow of the
College, on the question of Shakespeare's merits
compared with those of classical poets. The judges
who presided over "this ingenious assembly" unan-
imously and without qualification decided in favour
of Shakespeare's superiority.

A very eminent representative of the culture
and political intelligence of the next generation was

in full sympathy with the verdict of the Eton College
tribunal. Lord Clarendon held Shakespeare to be
one of the "most illustrious of our nation." Among
the many heroes of his admiration, Shakespeare
was of the elect few who were "most agreeable to
his lordship's general humour." Lord Clarendon
was at the pains of securing a portrait of Shakespeare to hang in his house in St. James's. Similarly,
the proudest and probably the richest nobleman
in political circles at the end of the seventeenth
century, the Duke of Somerset, was often heard to
speak of his "pleasure in that Greatness of Thought,
those natural Images, those Passions finely touch'd,
and that beautiful Expression which is everywhere
to be met with in Shakespear."

VIII

It was to this Duke of Somerset that Rowe
appropriately dedicated the first full and formal
biography of the poet. That work was designed
as a preface to the first critical edition of Shakespeare's plays, which Rowe published in 1709.
"Though the works of Mr Shakespear may seem
to many not to want a comment," Rowe wrote
modestly enough, "yet I fancy some little account
of the man himself may not be thought improper
to go along with them." Rowe did his work quite
as well as the rudimentary state of the biographic
art of his day allowed. He was under the complacent impression that his supply of information
satisfied all reasonable curiosity. He had placed
himself in the hands of Betterton, an investigator
at first hand. But the fact remains that Rowe

made no sustained nor scholarly effort to collect
exhaustively even the oral tradition; still less did he
consult with thoroughness official records or references to Shakespeare's literary achievements in the
books of his contemporaries. Such labour as that
was to be undertaken later, when the practice of
biography had assimilated more scientific method.
Rowe preferred the straw of vague rhapsody to
the brick of solid fact.

Nevertheless Rowe's memoir laid the foundations on which his successors built. It set ringing
the bell which called together that mass of information drawn from every source—manuscript archives,
printed books, oral tradition—which now far exceeds what is accessible in the case of any poet
contemporary with Shakespeare. Some links in
the chain of Shakespeare's career are still missing,
and we must wait for the future to disclose them.
But, though the clues at present are in some
places faint, the trail never altogether eludes the
patient investigator. The ascertained facts are
already numerous enough to define beyond risk of
intelligent doubt the direction that Shakespeare's
career followed. Its general outline is, as we have
seen, fully established by one source of knowledge
alone—one out of many—by the oral tradition
which survives from the seventeenth century.

It may be justifiable to cherish regret for the
loss of Shakespeare's autograph papers and of his
familiar correspondence. But the absence of such
documentary material can excite scepticism of the
received tradition only in those who are ignorant of
the fate that invariably befell the original manuscripts and correspondence of Elizabethan and

Jacobean poets and dramatists. Save for a few fragments of small literary moment, no play of the era in its writer's autograph escaped early destruction by fire or dustbin. No machinery then ensured, no custom then encouraged, the due preservation of the autographs of men distinguished for poetic genius. Provision was made in the public record offices or in private muniment-rooms for the protection of the official papers and correspondence of men in public life, and of manuscript memorials affecting the property and domestic history of great county families. But even in the case of men of the sixteenth or seventeenth century in official life who, as often happened, devoted their leisure to literature, the autographs of their literary compositions have for the most part perished, and there usually only remain in the official depositories remnants of their writings about matters of official routine.

Not all those depositories, it is to be admitted, have yet been fully explored, and in some of them a more thorough search than has yet been undertaken may be expected to throw new light on Shakespeare's biography. Meanwhile, instead of mourning helplessly over the lack of material for a knowledge of Shakespeare's life, it becomes us to estimate aright what we have at our command, to study it closely in the light of the literary history of the epoch, and, while neglecting no opportunity of bettering our information, to recognise frankly the activity of the destroying agencies which have been at work from the outset. Then we shall wonder, not why we know so little, but why we know so much.

IV

PEPYS AND SHAKESPEARE [1]

I

In his capacity of playgoer, as indeed in almost every other capacity, Pepys presents himself to readers of his naïve diary as the incarnation, or the microcosm, of the average man. No other writer has pictured with the same lifelike precision and simplicity the average playgoer's sensations of pleasure or pain. Of the play and its performers Pepys records exactly what he thinks or feels. He usually takes a more lively interest in the acting and in the scenic and musical accessories than in the drama's literary quality. Subtlety is at any rate absent from his criticism. He is either bored or amused. The piece is either the best or the worst that he ever witnessed. His epithets are of the bluntest and are without modulation. Wiser than more professional dramatic critics, he avoids labouring at reasons for his emphatic judgments.

Always true to his rôle of the average man, Pepys suffers his mind to be swayed by barely relevant accidents. His thought is rarely free from official

---

[1] A paper read at the sixth meeting of the Samuel Pepys Club, on Thursday, November 30, 1905, and printed in the *Fortnightly Review* for January, 1906.

or domestic business, and the heaviness or lightness
of his personal cares commonly colours his playhouse impressions. His praises and his censures of
a piece often reflect, too, the physical comforts or
discomforts which attach to his seat in the theatre.
He is peculiarly sensitive to petty annoyances—to
the agony of sitting in a draught, or to the irritation caused by frivolous talk in his near neighbourhood while a serious play is in progress. On one
occasion, when he sought to practise a praiseworthy
economy by taking a back seat in the shilling gallery
his evening's enjoyment was well-nigh spoiled by
finding the gaze of four clerks in his office steadily
directed upon him from more expensive seats down
below. On another occasion, when in the pit with
his wife and her waiting-woman, he was overcome
by a sense of shame as he realised how shabbily
his companions were dressed, in comparison with
the smartly-attired ladies round about them.

Everyone knows how susceptible Pepys was in
all situations of life to female charms. It was inevitable that his wits should often wander from
the dramatic theme and its scenic presentation to
the features of some woman on the stage or in the
auditory. An actress's pretty face or graceful figure many times diverted his attention from her
professional incompetence. It is doubtful if there
were any affront which Pepys would not pardon in
a pretty woman. Once when he was in the pit,
this curious experience befell him. "I sitting behind in a dark place," he writes, "a lady spit back-
ward upon me by mistake, not seeing me; but after
seeing her to be a very pretty lady, I was not
troubled at it at all." The volatile diarist studied

much besides the drama when he spent his afternoon or evening at the play.

Never was there a more indefatigable playgoer
than Pepys. Yet his enthusiasm for the theatre
was, to his mind, a failing which required most
careful watching. He feared that the passion might
do injury to his purse, might distract him from
serious business, might lead him into temptation
of the flesh. He had a little of the Puritan's dread
of the playhouse. He was constantly taking vows
to curb his love of plays, which "mightily troubled
his mind." He was frequently resolving to abstain
from the theatre for four or five months at a stretch,
and then to go only in the company of his wife.
During these periods of abstinence he was in the
habit of reading over his vows every Sunday. But,
in spite of all his well-meaning efforts, his resolution was constantly breaking down. On one occasion he perjured himself so thoroughly as to
witness two plays in one day, once in the afternoon
and again in the evening. On this riotous outbreak
he makes the characteristic comment: "Sad to
think of the spending so much money, and of ventur-
ing the breach of my vow." But he goes on to
thank God that he had the grace to feel sorry for
the misdeed, at the same time as he lamented that
"his nature was so content to follow the pleasure
still." Pepys compounded with his conscience for
such breaches of his oath by all manner of casuistry.
He excused himself for going, contrary to his vow,
to the new theatre in Drury Lane, because it was
not built when his vow was framed. Finally, he
stipulated with himself that he would only go to
the theatre once a fortnight; but if he went oftener he

would give £10 to the poor. "This," he added,
" I hope in God will bind me." The last reference
that he makes to his vows is when, in contraven-
tion of them, he went with his wife to the Duke of
York's House, and found the place full, and himself
unable to obtain seats. He makes a final record
of "the saving of his vow, to his great content."

II

All self-imposed restrictions notwithstanding,
Pepys contrived to visit the theatre no less than
three hundred and fifty-one times during the nine
years and five months that he kept his diary. It
has to be borne in mind that, for more than twelve
months of that period, the London playhouses were
for the most part closed, owing to the Great Plague
and the Fire. Had Pepys gone at regular intervals,
when the theatres were open, he would have been
a playgoer at least once a week. But, owing to his
vows, his visits fell at most irregular intervals.
Sometimes he went three or four times a week, or
even twice in one day. Then there would follow
eight or nine weeks of abstinence. If a piece especially took his fancy, he would see it six or seven
times in fairly quick succession. Long runs were
unknown to the theatre of Pepys's day, but a successful piece was frequently revived. Occasionally,
Pepys would put himself to the trouble of attending
a first night. But this was an indulgence that he
practised sparingly. He resented the manager's
habit of doubling the price of the seats, and he was
irritated by the frequent want of adequate rehearsal.

Pepys's theatrical experience began with the reopening of theatres after the severe penalty of sup-

pression, which the Civil Wars and the Commonwealth imposed on them for nearly eighteen years.
His playgoing diary thus became an invaluable
record of a new birth of theatrical life in London.
When, in the summer of 1660, General Monk occupied London for the restored King, Charles II.,
three of the old theatres were still standing empty.
These were soon put into repair, and applied anew
to theatrical uses, although only two of them seem
to have been open at any one time. The three
houses were the Red Bull, dating from Elizabeth's
reign, in St John's Street, Clerkenwell, where Pepys
saw Marlowe's *Faustus;* Salisbury Court, White-
friars, off Fleet Street; and the Old Cockpit in Drury
Lane, both of which were of more recent origin. To
all these theatres Pepys paid early visits. But the
Cockpit in Drury Lane, was the scene of some of his
most stirring experiences. There he saw his first play,
Beaumont and Fletcher's *Loyal Subject;* and there,
too, he saw his first play by Shakespeare, *Othello.*

But these three theatres were in decay, and new
and sumptuous buildings soon took their places.
One of the new playhouses was in Portugal Row,
Lincoln's Inn Fields; the other, on the site of the
present Drury Lane Theatre, was the first of the
many playhouses that sprang up there. It is to
these two theatres—Lincoln's Inn Fields and Drury
Lane—that Pepys in his diary most often refers.
He calls each of them by many different names,
and the unwary reader might infer that London was
very richly supplied with playhouses in Pepys's
day. But public theatres in active work at this
period of our history were not permitted by the
authorities to exceed two. "The Opera" and "the

Duke's House" are merely Pepys's alternative designations of the Lincoln's Inn Fields Theatre; while "the Theatre," "Theatre Royal," and "the King's House," are the varying titles which he bestows on the Drury Lane Theatre.[1]

Besides these two public theatres there was, in the final constitution of the theatrical world in Pepys's London, a third, which stood on a different footing. A theatre was attached to the King's Court at Whitehall, and there performances were given at the King's command by actors from the two public houses.[2] The private Whitehall theatre was open to the public on payment, and Pepys was frequently there.

At one period of his life Pepys held that his vows did not apply to the Court theatre, which was mainly distinguished from the other houses by the circumstances that the performances were given at night. At Lincoln's Inn Fields or Drury Lane it was only permitted to perform in the afternoon. Half-past three was the usual hour for opening the proceed-

---

[1] At the restoration of King Charles II., no more than two companies of actors received licenses to perform in public. One of these companies was directed by Sir William D'Avenant, Shakespeare's reputed godson, and was under the patronage of the King's brother, the Duke of York. The other was directed by Tom Killigrew, one of Charles II.'s boon companions, and was under the patronage of the King himself. In due time the Duke's, or D'Avenant's, company occupied the theatre in Lincoln's Inn Fields, and the King's, or Killigrew's, company occupied the new building in Drury Lane.

[2] Charles II. formed this private theatre out of a detached building in St. James's Park, known as the " Cockpit," and to be carefully distinguished from the Cockpit of Drury Lane. Part of the edifice was occupied by courtiers by favour of the King. General Monk had lodgings there. At a much later date, cabinet councils were often held there.

ings.   At Whitehall the play began about eight,
and often lasted till near midnight.

The general organisation of Pepys's auditorium
was much as it is to-day.   It had improved in many
particulars since Shakespeare died.   The pit was
the most popular part of the house; it covered the
floor of the building, and was provided with seats;
the price of admission was 2s. 6d.   The company
there seems to have been extremely mixed; men
and women of fashion often rubbed elbows with
City shopkeepers, their wives, and apprentices.
The first gallery was wholly occupied by boxes, in
which seats could be hired separately at 4s. apiece.
Above the boxes was the middle gallery, the central
part of which was filled with benches, where the seats
cost 1s. 6d. each, while boxes lined the sides.   The
highest tier was the 1s. gallery, where footmen soon
held sway.   As Pepys's fortune improved, he spent
more on his place in the theatre.   From the 1s.
gallery he descended to the 1s. 6d., and thence came
down to the pit, occasionally ascending to the boxes
on the first tier.

In the methods of representation, Pepys's period
of play-going was coeval with many most important
innovations, which seriously affected the presentation of Shakespeare on the stage.   The chief was
the desirable substitution of women for boys in the
female rôles.   During the first few months of Pepys's
theatrical experience, boys were still taking the
women's parts.   That the practice survived in the
first days of Charles II.'s reign we know from the
well-worn anecdote that when the King sent behind
the scenes to inquire why the play of *Hamlet*, which
he had come to see, was so late in commencing, he

was answered that the Queen was not yet shaved. But in the opening month of 1661, within five months of Pepys's first visit to a theatre, the reign of the boys ended. On January 3rd of that year, Pepys writes that he "first saw women come upon the stage." Next night he makes entry of a boy's performance of a woman's part, and that was the final record of boys masquerading as women in the English theatre. I believe the practice now survives nowhere except in Japan. This mode of representation has always been a great puzzle to students of Elizabethan drama.[1] Before, however, Pepys saw Shakespeare's work on the stage, the usurpation of the boys was over.

It was after the Restoration, too, that scenery, rich costume, and scenic machinery became, to Pepys's delight, regular features of the theatre. When the diarist saw *Hamlet* "done with scenes" for the first time, he was most favourably impressed. Musical accompaniment was known to pre-Restoration days; but the orchestra was now for the first time placed on the floor of the house in front of the stage, instead of in a side gallery, or on the stage itself. The musical accompaniment of plays developed very rapidly, and the methods of opera were soon applied to many of Shakespeare's pieces, notably to *The Tempest* and *Macbeth*.

Yet at the side of these innovations, one very important feature of the old playhouses, which gravely concerned both actors and auditors, survived throughout Pepys's lifetime. The stage still projected far into the pit in front of the curtain. The actors and actresses spoke in the centre of the house,

[1] For a fuller description of this theatrical practice see pages 41–43 *supra*.

so that, as Colley Cibber put it, "the most distant ear had scarce the least doubt or difficulty in hearing what fell from the weakest utterance . . . nor was the minutest motion of a feature, properly changing with the passion or humour it suited, ever lost, as they frequently must be, in the obscurity of too great a distance." The platform-stage, with which Shakespeare was familiar, suffered no curtailment in the English theatres till the eighteenth century, when the fore-edge of the boards was for the first time made to run level with the proscenium.

III

One of the obvious results of the long suppression of the theatres during the Civil Wars and Commonwealth was the temporary extinction of play-writing in England. On the sudden reopening of the playhouses at the Restoration, the managers had mainly to rely for sustenance on the drama of a long-past age. Of the one hundred and forty-five separate plays which Pepys witnessed, fully half belonged to the great period of dramatic activity in England, which covered the reigns of Elizabeth, James I., and Charles I. John Evelyn's well-known remark in his *Diary* (November 26, 1661): "I saw *Hamlet, Prince of Denmark*, played; but now the old plays begin to disgust this refined age," requires much qualification before it can be made to apply to Pepys's records of playgoing. It was in "the old plays" that he and all average playgoers mainly delighted.

Not that the new demand failed quickly to create a supply of new plays for the stage. Dryden and D'Avenant, the chief dramatists of Pepys's day, were rapid writers. To a large extent they carried on, with exaggeration of its defects and diminution of its merits, the old Elizabethan tradition of heroic romance, tragedy, and farce. The more matter-of-fact and lower-principled comedy of manners, which is commonly reckoned the chief characteristic of the new era in theatrical history, was only just beginning when Pepys was reaching the end of his diary. The virtual leaders of the new movement—Wycherley, Vanbrugh, Farquhar, and Congreve—were not at work till long after Pepys ceased to write. He records only the first runnings of that sparkling stream. He witnessed some impudent comedies of Dryden, Etherege, and Sedley. But it is important to note that he formed a low opinion of all of them. Their intellectual glitter did not appeal to him. Their cynical licentiousness seemed to him to be merely "silly." One might have anticipated from him a different verdict on the frank obscenity of Restoration drama. But there are the facts. Neither did Mr Pepys, nor (he is careful to remind us) did Mrs Pepys, take "any manner of pleasure in" the bold indelicacy of Dryden, Etherege, or Sedley.

When we ask what sort of pieces Pepys appreciated, we seem to be faced by further perplexities. His highest enthusiasm was evoked by certain plays of Ben Jonson, of Beaumont and Fletcher, and of Massinger. Near the zenith of his scale of dramatic excellence he set the comedies of Ben Jonson, which are remarkable for their portrayal of eccentricity of character. These pieces, which incline to farce, give great opportunity to what is commonly called character-acting, and character-acting always appeals most directly to average humanity. Pepys

called Jonson's *Alchemist* "a most incomparable
play," and he found in *Every Man in his Humour*
"the greatest propriety of speech that ever I read
in my life." Similarly, both the heroic tragedies
and the comedies of Beaumont and Fletcher, of
which he saw no less than nineteen, roused in him,
as a rule, an ecstatic admiration. But of all dramatic entertainments which the theatre offered him,
Pepys was most "taken" by the romantic comedy
from the pen of Massinger, which is called *The
Bondman*. "There is nothing more taking in the
world with me than that play," he writes.

Massinger's *Bondman* is a well-written piece, in
which an heroic interest is fused with a genuine
spirit of low comedy. Yet Pepys's unqualified
commendation of it presents a problem. Massinger's play, like the cognate work of Fletcher, offers
much episode which is hardly less indecent than
those early specimens of Restoration comedy of
which Pepys disapproved. A leading character is
a frowsy wife who faces all manner of humiliation,
in order to enjoy, behind her elderly husband's
back, the embraces of a good-looking youth.

Pepys is scarcely less tolerant of Fletcher's more
flagrant infringements of propriety. In the whole
of the Elizabethan drama there was no piece which
presented so liberal a mass of indelicacy as Fletcher's
Custom of the Country. Dryden, who was innocent
of prudery, declared that there was "more in-
decency" in that drama "than in all our plays together." This was one of the pieces which Pepys
twice saw performed after carefully reading it in
his study, and he expressed admiration for the
rendering of the widow's part by his pretty friend,

Mistress Knipp. One has to admit that Pepys condemned the play from a literary point of view as "a very poor one, methinks," as "fully the worst play that I saw or believe shall see." But the pleasure which Mistress Knipp's share in the performance gave him suggests, in the absence of any explicit disclaimer, that the improprieties of both plot and characters escaped his notice, or, at any rate, excited in him no disgust. Massinger's *Bondman*, Pepys's ideal of merit in drama, has little of the excessive grossness of the *Custom of the Country*. But to some extent it is tarred with the same brush.

Pepys's easy principles never lend themselves to very strict definition. Yet he may be credited with a certain measure of discernment in pardoning the indelicacy of Fletcher and Massinger, while he condemns that of Dryden, Etherege, or Sedley. Indelicacy in the older dramatists does not ignore worthier interests. Other topics attracted the earlier writers besides conjugal infidelity and the frailty of virgins, which were the sole themes of Restoration comedy. Massinger's heroes are not always gay seducers. His husbands are not always fools. Pepys might quite consistently scorn the ribaldry of Etherege and condone the obscenity of Fletcher. It was a question of degree. Pepys was clear in his own mind that a line must be drawn somewhere, though it would probably have taxed his logical power to make the delimitation precise.

IV

There is, apparently, a crowning difficulty of far greater moment when finally estimating Pepys's taste in dramatic literature. Despite his admiration for the ancient drama, he acknowledged a very tempered regard for the greatest of all the old dramatists—Shakespeare. He lived and died in complacent unconsciousness of Shakespeare's supreme excellence. Such innocence is attested by his conduct outside, as well as inside, the theatre. He prided himself on his taste as a reader and a book collector, and bought for his library many plays in quarto which he diligently perused. Numerous separately issued pieces by Shakespeare lay at his disposal in the bookshops. But he only records the purchase of one—the first part of *Henry IV.*, though he mentions that he read in addition *Othello* and *Hamlet*. When his bookseller first offered him the great First Folio edition of Shakespeare's works, he rejected it for Fuller's *Worthies* and the newly-published Butler's *Hudibras*, in which, by the way, he failed to discover the wit. Ultimately he bought the newly-issued second impression of the Third Folio Shakespeare, along with copies of Spelman's *Glossary* and Scapula's *Lexicon*. To these soporific works of reference he apparently regarded the dramatist's volume as a fitting pendant. He seemed subsequently to have exchanged the Third Folio for a Fourth, by which volume alone is Shakespeare represented in the extant library that Pepys bequeathed to Magdalene College, Cambridge.

As a regular playgoer at a time when the stage mainly depended on the drama of Elizabethan days, Pepys was bound to witness numerous performances of Shakespeare's plays. On the occasion of forty-one of his three hundred and fifty-one visits to the theatre, Pepys listened to plays by Shakespeare, or to pieces based upon them. Once in every eight performances Shakespeare was presented to his view. Fourteen was the number of different plays by Shakespeare which Pepys saw during these forty-one visits. Very few caused him genuine pleasure. At least three he condemns, without any qualification, as "tedious," or "silly." In the case of others, while he ignored the literary merit, he enjoyed the scenery and music with which, in accordance with current fashion, the dramatic poetry was overlaid. In only two cases, in the case of two tragedies— *Othello* and *Hamlet*—does he show at any time a true appreciation of the dramatic quality, and in the case of *Othello* he came in course of years to abandon his good opinion.

Pepys's moderate praise and immoderate blame of Shakespeare are only superficially puzzling. The ultimate solution is not difficult. Despite his love of music and his zeal as a collector, Pepys was the most matter-of-fact of men; he was essentially a man of business. Not that he had any distaste for timely recreation; he was, indeed, readily susceptible to every manner of commonplace pleasures—to all the delights of both mind and sense which appeal to the practical and hard-headed type of Englishman. Things of the imagination, on the other hand, stood with him on a different footing. They were out of his range or sphere. Poetry and romance, unless liberally compounded with prosaic ingredients, bored him on the stage and elsewhere.

In the plays of Beaumont and Fletcher, of Massinger and Ben Jonson, poetry and romance were for the most part kept in the background. Such elements lay there behind a substantial barrier of conventional stage machinery and elocutionary scaffolding. In Shakespeare, poetry and romance usually eluded the mechanical restrictions of the theatre. The gold had a tendency to separate itself from the alloy, and Pepys only found poetry and romance endurable when they were pretty thickly veiled behind the commonplaces of rhetoric, or broad fun, or the realistic ingenuity of the stage carpenter and upholsterer.

There is, consequently, no cause for surprise that Pepys should write thus of Shakespeare's ethereal comedy of *A Midsummer Night's Dream:* "Then to the King's Theatre, where we saw *Midsummer Night's Dream*, which I had never seen before, nor shall ever again, for it is the most insipid, ridiculous play that ever I saw in my life. I saw, I confess, some good dancing and some handsome women, which was all my pleasure." This is Pepys's ordinary attitude of mind to undiluted poetry on the stage.

Pepys only saw *A Midsummer Night's Dream* once. *Twelfth Night*, of which he wrote in very similar strains, he saw thrice. On the first occasion his impatience of this romantic play was due to external causes. He went to the theatre "against his own mind and resolution." He was over-persuaded to go in by a friend, with whom he was casually walking past the house in Lincoln's Inn Fields. Moreover, he had just sworn to his wife that he would never go to a play without her: all which considerations "made the piece seem a burden" to him. He witnessed *Twelfth Night* twice again in a less perturbed spirit, and then he called it a "silly" play, or "one of the weakest plays that ever I saw on the stage."

Again, of *Romeo and Juliet*, Pepys wrote: "It is

a play of itself the worst I ever heard in my life."
This verdict, it is right to add, was attributable, in
part at least, to Pepys's irritation at the badness
of the acting, and at the actors' ignorance of their
words. It was a first night.

The literary critic knows well enough that the
merit of these three pieces—*A Midsummer Night's
Dream, Twelfth Night*, and *Romeo and Juliet*—
mainly lies in their varied wealth of poetic imagery
and passion. One thing alone could render the
words, in which poetic genius finds voice, tolerable
in the playhouse to a spectator of Pepys's prosaic
temperament. The one thing needful is inspired acting, and in the case of these three plays, when Pepys
saw them performed, inspired acting was wanting.

It is at first sight disconcerting to find Pepys no
less impatient of *The Merry Wives of Windsor.*
He expresses a mild interest in the humours of
"the country gentleman and the French doctor."
But he condemns the play as a whole. It is in
his favour that his bitterest reproaches are aimed at
the actors and actresses. One can hardly conceive
that Falstaff, fitly interpreted, would have failed
to satisfy Pepys's taste in humour, commonplace
though it was. He is not quite explicit on the
point; but there are signs that the histrionic interpretation of Shakespeare's colossal humorist, rather
than the dramatist's portrayal of the character,
caused the diarist's disappointment.

Just before Pepys saw the first part of *Henry
IV.*, wherein Falstaff figures to supreme advantage,
he had bought and read the play in quarto. "But
my expectation being too great" (he avers), "it did
not please me as otherwise I believe it would."

Here it seems clear that his hopes of the actor were unfulfilled. However, he saw *Henry IV.* again a few months later, and had the grace to describe it as "a good play." On a third occasion he wrote that, "contrary to expectation," he was pleased by the delivery of Falstaff's ironical speech about honour. For whatever reason, Pepys's affection for Shakespeare's fat knight, as he figured on the stage of his day, never touched the note of exaltation.

Of Shakespeare's great tragedies Pepys saw three —*Othello*, *Hamlet*, and *Macbeth*. But in considering his several impressions of these pieces, we have to make an important proviso. Only the first two of them did he witness in the authentic version. *Macbeth* underwent in his day a most liberal transformation, which carried it far from its primordial purity. The impressions he finally formed of *Othello* and *Hamlet* are not consistent one with the other, but are eminently characteristic of the variable moods of the average playgoer.

Othello he saw twice, and he tells us more of the acting than of the play itself. On his first visit he notes that the lady next him shrieked on seeing Desdemona smothered: a proof of the strength of the histrionic illusion. Up to the year 1666 Pepys adhered to the praiseworthy opinion that *Othello* was a "mighty good" play. But in that year his judgment took a turn for the worse, and that for a reason which finally convicts him of incapacity to pass just sentence on the poetic or literary drama. On August 20, 1666, he writes: "Read *Othello, Moor of Venice*, which I have ever heretofore esteemed a mighty good play; but having so lately read the *Adventures of Five Hours*, it seems a mean thing."

Most lovers of Shakespeare will agree that the great dramatist rarely showed his mature powers to more magnificent advantage than in his treatment of plot and character in *Othello*. What, then, is this *Adventures of Five Hours*, compared with which *Othello* became in Pepys's eyes "a mean thing"? It is a trivial comedy of intrigue, adapted from the Spanish by one Sir Samuel Tuke. A choleric guardian arranges for his ward, who also happens to be his sister, to marry against her will a man whom she has never seen. Without her guardian's knowledge she, before the design goes further, escapes with a lover of her own choosing. In her place she leaves a close friend, who is wooed in mistake for herself by the suitor destined for her own hand. This is the main dramatic point; the thread is very slender, and is drawn out to its utmost limits through five acts of blank verse. The language and metre are scrupulously correct. But one cannot credit the play with any touch of poetry or imagination. It presents a trite theme tamely and prosaically. Congenital inability of the most inveterate toughness to appreciate dramatic poetry could alone account for a mention of the *Adventures of Five Hours* in the same breath with *Othello*.

Pepys did not again fall so low as this. The only other tragedy of Shakespeare which he saw in its authentic purity moved him, contradictorily, to transports of unqualified delight. One is glad to recall that *Hamlet*, one of the greatest of Shakespeare's plays, received from Pepys ungrudging commendation. Pepys's favourable opinion of *Hamlet* is to be assigned to two causes. One is the literary and psychological attractions of the piece; the other, and perhaps the more important, is the manner in which the play was interpreted on the stage of Pepys's time.

Pepys is not the only owner of a prosaic mind who has found satisfaction in Shakespeare's portrait of the Prince of Denmark. Over minds of almost every calibre, that hero of the stage has always exerted a pathetic fascination, which natural antipathy to poetry seems unable to extinguish. Pepys's testimony to his respect for the piece is abundant. The whole of one Sunday afternoon (November 13, 1664), he spent at home with his wife, "getting a speech out of *Hamlet*, 'To be or not to be,' without book." He proved, indeed, his singular admiration for those familiar lines in a manner which I believe to be unique. He set them to music, and the notes are extant in a book of manuscript music in his library at Magdalene College, Cambridge. The piece is a finely-elaborated recitative fully equal to the requirements of grand opera. The composer gives intelligent and dignified expression to every word of the soliloquy. Very impressive is the modulation of the musical accompaniment to the lines—

> To die, to sleep!
> To sleep, perchance to dream! ay, there's the rub.

It is possible that the cadences of this musical rendering of Hamlet's speech preserve some echo of the intonation of the great actor, Betterton, whose performance evoked in Pepys lasting adoration.[1]

It goes without saying that, for the full enjoy-

[1] Sir Frederick Bridge, by permission of the Master and Fellows of Magdalene College, Cambridge, caused this setting of " To be or not to be " (which bears no composer's signature) to be transcribed from the manuscript, and he arranged the piece to be sung at the meeting of the Pepys Club on November 30, 1905. Sir Frederick Bridge believes Pepys to be the composer.

ment of a performance of *Hamlet* by both cultured and uncultured spectators, acting of supreme quality is needful. Luckily for Pepys, Hamlet in his day was rendered by an actor who, according to ample extant testimony, interpreted the part to perfection. Pepys records four performances of *Hamlet*, with Betterton in the title-rôle on each occasion. With every performance Pepys's enthusiasm rose. The first time he writes (August 24, 1661): "Saw the play done with scenes very well at the Opera, but above all Betterton did the Prince's part beyond imagination." On the third occasion (May 28, 1663), the rendering gave him "fresh reason never to think enough of Betterton." On the last occasion (August 31, 1668) he was "mightily pleased," but above all with Betterton, "the best part, I believe, that ever man acted."

Hamlet was one of the most popular plays of Pepys's day, mainly owing to Betterton's extraordinary faculty. The history of the impersonation presents numerous points of the deepest interest. The actor was originally coached in the part by D'Avenant. The latter is said to have derived hints for the rendering from an old actor, Joseph Taylor, who had played the rôle in Shakespeare's own day, and had been instructed in it by the dramatist himself. This tradition gives additional value to Pepys's musical setting in recitative of the "To be or not to be" soliloquy. If we accept the reasonable theory that that piece of music preserves something of the cadences of Betterton's enunciation, it is no extravagance to suggest that a note here or there enshrines the modulation of the voice of Shakespeare himself. For there is the likelihood that

the dramatist was Betterton's instructor at no
more than two removes. Only the lips of D'Avenant, Shakespeare's godson, and of Taylor, Shakespeare's acting colleague, intervened between the
dramatist and the Hamlet of Pepys's diary. Those
alone, who have heard the musical setting of "To
be or not to be" adequately rendered, are in a
position to reject this hypothesis altogether.

Among seventeenth century critics there was
unanimous agreement—a rare thing among dramatic
critics of any period—as to the merits of Betterton's
performance. In regard to his supreme excellence,
men of the different mental calibre of Sir Richard
Steele, Colley Cibber, and Nicholas Rowe, knew no
difference of opinion. According to Cibber, Betterton invariably preserved the happy "medium
between mouthing and meaning too little"; he held
the attention of the audience by "a tempered spirit,"
not by mere vehemence of voice. His solemn,
trembling voice made the Ghost equally terrible to
the spectator and to himself. Another critic relates
that when Betterton's Hamlet saw the Ghost in his
mother's chamber, the actor turned as pale as his
neckcloth; every joint of his body seemed to be affected with a tremor inexpressible, and the audience
shared his astonishment and horror. Nicholas Rowe
declared that "Betterton performed the part as if it
had been written on purpose for him, as if the author
had conceived it as he played it." It is difficult to
imagine any loftier commendation of a Shakespearean
player.

V

There is little reason to doubt that the plays of
Shakespeare which I have enumerated were all seen

by Pepys in authentic shapes. Betterton acted Lear, we are positively informed, "exactly as Shakespeare wrote it"; and at the dates when Pepys saw *Hamlet, Twelfth Night,* and the rest, there is no evidence that the old texts had been tampered with. The rage for adapting Shakespeare to current theatrical requirements reached its full tide after the period of Pepys's diary. Pepys witnessed only the first-fruits of that fantastic movement. It acquired its greatest luxuriance later. The pioneer of the great scheme of adaptation was Sir William D'Avenant, and he was aided in Pepys's playgoing days by no less a personage than Dryden. It was during the succeeding decade that the scandal, fanned by the energies of lesser men, was at its unseemly height.

No disrespect seems to have been intended to Shakespeare's memory by those who devoted themselves to these acts of vandalism. However difficult it may be to realise the fact, true admiration for Shakespeare's genius seems to have flourished in the breasts of all the adapters, great and small. D'Avenant, whose earliest poetic production was a pathetic elegy on the mighty dramatist, never ceased to write or speak of him with the most affectionate respect. Dryden, who was first taught by D'Avenant "to admire" Shakespeare's work, attests in his critical writings a reverence for its unique excellence, which must satisfy the most enthusiastic worshipper. The same temper characterises references to Shakespeare on the part of dramatists of the Restoration, who brought to the adaptation of Shakespeare abilities of an order far inferior to those of Dryden or of D'Avenant. Nahum Tate, one of the least respected names in English literature, was one of the freest adapters of Shakespearean drama to the depraved taste of the day. Yet even he assigned to the master playwright unrivalled insight into the darkest mysteries of human nature, and an absolute mastery of the faculty of accurate characterisation. For once, Tate's literary judgment must go unquestioned.

It was no feeling of disrespect or of dislike for Shakespeare's work—it was the change that was taking place in the methods of theatrical representation, which mainly incited the Shakespearean adapters of the Restoration to their benighted labours. Shakespeare had been acted without scenery or musical accompaniment. As soon as scenic machinery and music had become ordinary accessories of the stage, it seemed to theatrical managers almost a point of honour to fit Shakespearean drama to the new conditions. To abandon him altogether was sacrilege. Yet the mutation of public taste offered, as the only alternative to his abandonment, the obligation of bestowing on his work every mechanical advantage, every tawdry ornament in the latest mode.

Pepys fully approved the innovations, and two of the earliest of Shakespearean adaptations won his unqualified eulogy. These were D'Avenant's reconstructions of *The Tempest* and *Macbeth*. D'Avenant had convinced himself that both plays readily lent themselves to spectacle; they would repay the embellishments of ballets, new songs, new music, coloured lights, and flying machines. Reinforced by these charms of novelty, the old pieces might enjoy an everlasting youth. No spectator more

ardently applauded such bastard sentiment than
the playgoing Pepys.

Of the two pieces, the text of *Macbeth* was
abbreviated, but otherwise the alterations in the
blank-verse speeches were comparatively slight.   Additional songs were provided for the Witches, together with much capering in the air.   Music was
specially written by Matthew Locke.   The liberal
introduction of song and dance rendered the piece,
in Pepys's strange phrase, "a most excellent play
for variety."   He saw D'Avenant's version of it no
less than eight times, with ever-increasing enjoyment.   He generously praised the clever combina-
tion of "a deep tragedy with a divertissement."
He detected no incongruity in the amalgamation.
"Though I have seen it often," he wrote later, "yet
is it one of the best plays for a stage, and for variety
of dancing and music, that ever I saw."

The Tempest, the other adapted play, which is
prominent in Pepys's diary, underwent more drastic
revision.   Here D'Avenant had the co-operation of
Dryden; and no intelligent reader can hesitate to
affirm that the ingenuity of these worthies ruined
this splendid manifestation of poetic fancy and insight.   It is only fair to Dryden to add that he dis-
claimed any satisfaction in his share in the outrage.
The first edition of the barbarous revision was first
published in 1670, after D'Avenant's death, and
Dryden wrote a preface, in which he prudently
remarked: "I do not set a value on anything I
have written in this play but [*i.e.*, except] out of
gratitude to the memory of Sir William Davenant,
who did me the honour to join me with him in the
alteration of it."

The numerous additions, for which the distinguished coadjutors are responsible, reek with mawkish sentimentality, inane vapidity, or vulgar buffoonery. Most of the leading characters are duplicated or triplicated. Miranda has a sister, Dorinda, who is repellently coquettish. This new creation finds a lover in another new character, a brainless youth, Hippolito, who has never before seen a woman. Caliban becomes the most sordid of clowns, and is allotted a sister, Milcha, who apes his coarse buffoonery. Ariel, too, is given a female associate, Sycorax, together with many attendants. The sailors are increased in number, and a phalanx of dancing devils join in their antics.

But the chief feature of the revived *Tempest* was the music, the elaborate scenery, and the scenic mechanism.¹ There was an orchestra of twenty-four violins in front of the stage, with harpsichords and "theorbos" to accompany the voices; new songs

¹ The Dryden-D'Avenant perversion of *The Tempest* which Pepys witnessed underwent a further deterioration in 1673, when Thomas Shadwell, poet laureate, to the immense delight of the playgoing public, rendered the piece's metamorphosis into an opera more complete. In 1674 the Dryden-D'Avenant edition was reissued, with Shadwell's textual and scenic amplification, although no indication was given on the title-page or elsewhere of his share in the venture. Contemporary histories of the stage make frequent reference to Shadwell's " Opera " of *The Tempest;* but no copy was known to be extant until Sir Ernest Clarke proved, in *The Athenæum* for 25th August 1906, that the second and later editions of the Dryden-D'Avenant version embodied Shadwell's operatic embellishments, and are copies of what was known in theatrical circles of the day as Shadwell's " Opera." Shadwell's stage-directions are more elaborate than those of Dryden and D'Avenant, and there are other minor innovations; but there is little difference in the general design of the two versions. Shadwell merely bettered Dryden's and D'Avenant's instructions.

were dispersed about the piece with unsparing hand. The curious new "Echo" song in Act III.—a duet between Ferdinand and Ariel—was deemed by Pepys to be so "mighty pretty" that he requested the composer—Bannister—to "prick him down the notes." Many times did the audience shout with joy as Ariel, with a *corps de ballet* in attendance, winged his flight to the roof of the stage.

The scenic devices which distinguished the Restoration production of *The Tempest* have, indeed, hardly been excelled for ingenuity in our own day. The arrangements for the sinking of the ship in the first scene would do no discredit to the spectacular magnificence of the London stage of our own day. The scene represented "a thick cloudy sky, a very rocky coast, and a tempestuous sea in perpetual agitation." "This tempest," according to the stage-directions, "has many dreadful objects in it; several spirits in horrid shapes flying down among the sailors, then rising and crossing in the air; and when the ship is sinking, the whole house is darkened and a shower of fire falls upon the vessel. This is accompanied by lightning and several claps of thunder till the end of the storm." The stage-manager's notes proceed:—"In the midst of the shower of fire, the scene changes. The cloudy sky, rocks, and sea vanish, and when the lights return, discover that beautiful part of the island, which was the habitation of Prospero: 'tis composed of three walks of cypress trees; each side-walk leads to a cave, in one of which Prospero keeps his daughter, in the other Hippolito (the interpolated character of the man who has never seen a woman). The middle walk is of great depth, and leads to an open part of the island." Every scene of the play was framed with equal elaborateness.

Pepys's comment on *The Tempest*, when he first witnessed its production in such magnificent conditions, runs thus:—"The play has no great wit but yet good above ordinary plays." Pepys subsequently, however, saw the piece no less than five times, and the effect of the music, dancing, and scenery, steadily grew upon him. On his second visit he wrote:—"Saw *The Tempest* again, which is very pleasant, and full of so good variety, that I cannot be more pleased almost in a comedy. Only the seamen's part a little too tedious." Finally, Pepys praised the richly-embellished *Tempest* without any sort of reserve, and took "pleasure to learn the tune of the seamen's dance."

Other adaptations of Shakespeare, which followed somewhat less spectacular methods of barbarism, roused in Pepys smaller enthusiasm. *The Rivals*, a version by D'Avenant of *The Two Noble Kinsmen* (the joint production of Fletcher and Shakespeare), was judged by Pepys to be "no excellent piece," though he appreciated the new songs, which included the familiar "My lodging is on the cold ground," with music by Matthew Locke. Pepys formed a higher opinion of D'Avenant's liberally-altered version of *Measure for Measure*, which the adapter called *The Law against Lovers*, and into which he introduced, with grotesque effect, the characters of Beatrice and Benedick from *Much Ado about Nothing*. But it is more to Pepys's credit that he bestowed a very qualified approval on an execrable adaptation by the actor Lacy of *The Taming of the Shrew*. Here the hero, Petruchio, is overshadowed by a new character, Sawney, his Scottish servant, who speaks an unintelligible *patois*. "It hath some very good pieces in it," writes Pepys, "but generally is but a mean play, and the best part, Sawny, done by Lacy, hath not half its life by reason of the words, I suppose, not being understood, at least by me."

VI

It might be profitable to compare Pepys's experiences as a spectator of Shakespeare's plays on the stage with the opportunities open to playgoers at the present moment. Modern managers have been producing Shakespearean drama of late with great liberality, and usually in much splendour. Neither the points of resemblance between the modern and the Pepysian methods, nor the points of difference, are flattering to the esteem of ourselves as a literature-loving people. It is true that we no longer garble our acting versions of Shakespeare. We are content with abbreviations of the text, some of which are essential, but many of which injure the dramatic perspective, and with inversion of scenes which may or may not be justifiable. But, to my mind, it is in our large dependence on scenery that we are following too closely that tradition of the Restoration which won the wholehearted approval of Pepys. The musico-scenic method of producing Shakespeare can always count on the applause of the average multitude of playgoers, of which Pepys is the ever-living spokesman. It is Shakespeare with scenic machinery, Shakespeare with new songs, Shakespeare with incidental music, Shakespeare with interpolated ballets, that reaches

the heart of the British public. If the average
British playgoer were gifted with Pepys's frankness,
I have little doubt that he would echo the diarist's
condemnation of Shakespeare in his poetic purity,
of Shakespeare as the mere interpreter of human
nature, of Shakespeare without flying machines, of
Shakespeare without song and dance; he would
characterise undiluted Shakespearean drama as "a
mean thing," or the most tedious entertainment that
ever he was at in his life.

But the situation in Pepys's day had, despite
all the perils that menaced it, a saving grace.
Great acting, inspired acting, is an essential condition to any general appreciation in the theatre
of Shakespeare's dramatic genius. However seduc-
tive may be the musico-scenic ornamentation,
Shakespeare will never justly affect the mind of the
average playgoer unless great or inspired actors are
at hand to interpret him. Luckily for Pepys, he
was the contemporary of at least one inspired Shakespearean actor. The exaltation of spirit to which he
confesses, when he witnessed Betterton in the rôle of
Hamlet, is proof that the prosaic multitude for whom
he speaks will always respond to Shakespeare's magic
touch when genius wields the actor's wand. One
could wish nothing better for the playgoing public of
to-day than that the spirit of Betterton, Shakespeare's guardian angel in the theatre of the Restoration, might renew its earthly career in our own
time in the person of some contemporary actor.

V

MR BENSON AND SHAKESPEAREAN DRAMA [1]

I

DRAMATIC criticism in the daily press of London often resembles that method of conversation of which Bacon wrote that it seeks "rather commendation of wit, in being able to hold argument, than of judgment, in discerning what is true." For four-and-twenty years, Mr F. R. Benson has directed an acting company which has achieved a reputation in English provincial cities, in Ireland, and in Scotland, by its exclusive devotion to Shakespearean and classical drama. Mr Benson's visits to London have been rare. There he has too often made sport for the journalistic censors who aim at "commendation of wit."

Even the best-intentioned of Mr Benson's critics in London have fallen into the habit of concentrating attention on unquestionable defects in Mr Benson's practice, to the neglect of the vital principles which are the justification of his policy. Mr Benson's principles have been largely ignored by the newspapers; but they are not wisely disregarded. They are matters of urgent public interest. They point

[1] This paper was first printed in the *Cornhill Magazine*, May, 1900.

the right road to the salvation of Shakespearean drama on the modern stage. They cannot be too often pressed on public notice.

These, in my view, are the five points of the charter which Mr Benson is and has long been championing with a persistency which claims national recognition.

Firstly, it is to the benefit of the nation that Shakespeare's plays should be acted constantly and in their variety.

Secondly, a theatrical manager who undertakes to produce Shakespearean drama should change his programme at frequent intervals, and should permit no long continuous run of any single play.

Thirdly, all the parts, whatever their significance, should be entrusted to exponents who have been trained in the delivery of blank verse, and have gained some knowledge and experience of the range of Shakespearean drama.

Fourthly, no play should be adapted by the manager so as to give greater prominence than the text invites to any single rôle.

Fifthly, the scenic embellishments should be simple and inexpensive, and should be subordinated to the dramatic interest.

There is no novelty in these principles. The majority of them were accepted unhesitatingly in the past by Betterton, Garrick, Edmund Kean, the Kembles, and notably by Phelps. They are recognised principles to-day in the leading theatres of France and Germany. But by some vagary of fate or public taste they have been reckoned in London, for a generation at any rate, to be out of date.

In the interest of the manager, the actor, and

the student, a return to the discarded methods has become, in the opinion of an influential section of the educated public, imperative. Mr Benson is the only manager of recent date to inscribe boldly and continuously on his banner the old watchwords: "Shakespeare and the National Drama," "Short Runs," "No Stars," "All-round Competence," and "Unostentatious Setting." What better title could be offered to the support and encouragement of the intelligent playgoer?

II

A constant change of programme, such as the old methods of the stage require, causes the present generation of London playgoers, to whom it is unfamiliar, a good deal of perplexity. Londoners have grown accustomed to estimate the merits of a play by the number of performances which are given of it in uninterrupted succession. They have forgotten how mechanical an exercise of the lungs and limbs acting easily becomes; how frequent repetition of poetic speeches, even in the most competent mouths, robs the lines of their poetic temper.

Numbness of intellect, rigidity of tone, artificiality of expression, are fatal alike to the enunciation of Shakespearean language and to the interpretation of Shakespearean character. The system of short runs, of the nightly alterations of the play, such as Mr Benson has revived, is the only sure preservative against maladies so fatal.

Hardly less important is Mr Benson's new-old principle of "casting" a play of Shakespeare. Not only in the leading rôles of Shakespeare's masterpieces, but in subordinate parts throughout the

range of his work, the highest abilities of the actor
can find some scope for employment. A competent
knowledge of the poet's complete work is needed to
bring this saving truth home to those who are engaged in presenting Shakespearean drama on the
stage. An actor hardly realises the real force of the
doctrine until he has had experience of the potential-
ities of a series of the smaller characters by making
practical endeavours to interpret them. Adequate
opportunities of the kind are only accessible to
members of a permanent company, whose energies
are absorbed in the production of the Shakespearean
drama constantly and in its variety, and whose
programme is untrammelled by the poisonous system of "long runs." Shakespearean actors should
drink deep of the Pierian spring. They should be
graduates in Shakespeare's university; and, unlike
graduates of other universities, they should master
not merely formal knowledge, but a flexible power
of using it.

Mr Benson's company is, I believe, the only one
at present in existence in England which confines
almost all its efforts to the acting of Shakespeare.
In the course of its twenty-four years' existence its
members have interpreted in the theatre no less than
thirty of Shakespeare's plays.[1] The natural result

[1] Mr Benson, writing to me on 13th January 1906, gives the
following list of plays by Shakespeare which he has produced:—
*Antony and Cleopatra, As You Like It, The Comedy of Errors,
Coriolanus, Hamlet, Henry IV. (Parts 1 and 2), Henry V.,
Henry VI. (Parts 1, 2, and 3), Henry VIII., Julius Cæsar, King
John, King Lear, Macbeth, The Merchant of Venice, The Merry
Wives of Windsor, A Midsummer Night's Dream, Much Ado
About Nothing, Othello, Pericles, Richard II., Richard III.,
Romeo and Juliet, The Taming of the Shrew, The Tempest,*

is that Mr Benson and his colleagues have learned in practice the varied calls that Shakespearean drama makes upon actors' capacities.

Members of Mr Benson's company have made excellent use of their opportunities. An actor, like the late Frank Rodney, who could on one night competently portray Bolingbroke in *Richard II.* and on the following night the clown Feste in *Twelfth Night* with equal effect, clearly realised something of the virtue of Shakespearean versatility. Mr Benson's leading comedian, Mr Weir, whose power of presenting Shakespeare's humorists shows, besides native gifts, the advantages that come of experienced study of the dramatist, not only interprets, in the genuine spirit, great rôles like Falstaff and Touchstone, but gives the truest possible significance to the comparatively unimportant rôles of the First Gardener in *Richard II.* and Grumio in *The Taming of the Shrew.*

Nothing could be more grateful to a student of Shakespeare than the manner in which the small part of John of Gaunt was played by Mr Warburton in Mr Benson's production of *Richard II.* The part includes the glorious panegyric of England which comes from the lips of the dying man, and must challenge the best efforts of every actor of ambition

Timon of Athens, Twelfth Night, and *A Winter's Tale.* Phelps's record only exceeded Mr Benson's by one. He produced thirty-one of Shakespeare's plays in all, but he omitted *Richard II.,* and the three parts of *Henry VI.,* which Mr Benson has acted, while he included *Love's Labour's Lost, The Two Gentlemen of Verona, All's Well that Ends Well, Cymbeline,* and *Measure for Measure,* which Mr Benson, so far, has eschewed. Mr Phelps and Mr Benson are at one in avoiding *Titus Andronicus* and *Troilus and Cressida.*

and self-respect. But in the mouth of an actor who
lacks knowledge of the true temper of Shakespearean
drama, this speech is certain to be mistaken for a
detached declamation of patriotism—an error which
ruins its dramatic significance. As Mr Warburton
delivered it, one listened to the despairing cry of a
feeble old man roused for a moment from the lethargy of sickness by despair at the thought that the
great country he loved was in peril of decay through
the selfish and frivolous temper of its ruler.   Instead
of a Chauvinist manifesto defiantly declaimed under
the limelight, there was offered us the quiet pathos of
a dying patriot's lament over his beloved country's
misfortunes—an oracular warning from a death-
stricken tongue, foreshadowing with rare solemnity
and dramatic irony the violent doom of the reckless
worker of the mischief. Any other conception of
the passage, any conscious endeavour to win a round
of applause by elocutionary display, would disable
the actor from doing justice to the great and sadly
stirring utterance. The right note could only be
sounded by one who was acclimatised to Shakespearean drama, and had recognised the wealth of
significance to be discovered and to be disclosed
(with due artistic restraint) in Shakespeare's minor
characters.

III

The benefits to be derived from the control of a
trained school of Shakespearean actors were displayed very conspicuously when Mr Benson undertook six years ago the heroic task of performing
the play of *Hamlet*, as Shakespeare wrote it, without
any abbreviation. *Hamlet* is the longest of Shake-

speare's plays; it reaches a total of over 3900 lines.
It is thus some 900 lines longer than *Antony and
Cleopatra,* which of all Shakespeare's plays most
nearly approaches its length. Consequently it is a
tradition of the stage to cut the play of *Hamlet* by
the omission of more than a third. Hamlet's part
is usually retained almost in its entirety, but the
speeches of every other character are seriously cur-
tailed. Mr Benson ventured on the bold innovation of giving the play in full.[1]

Only he who has witnessed the whole play on the
stage can fully appreciate its dramatic capabilities.
It is obvious that, in whatever shape the play of
Hamlet is produced in the theatre, its success must
always be primarily due to the overpowering fascination exerted on the audience by the character of
the hero. In every conceivable circumstance the
young prince must be the centre of attraction.
Nevertheless, no graver injury can be done the play
as an acting drama than by treating it as a one-part
piece. The accepted method of shortening the
tragedy by reducing every part, except that of
Hamlet, is to distort Shakespeare's whole scheme,
to dislocate or obscure the whole action. The pre-
dominance of Hamlet is exaggerated at the expense
of the dramatist's artistic purpose.

[1] The performance occupied nearly six hours. One half was
given in the afternoon, and the other half in the evening of the
same day, with an interval of an hour and a half between the
two sections. Should the performance be repeated, I would rec-
ommend, in the interests of busy men and women, that the whole
play be rendered at a single sitting, which might be timed to
open at a somewhat earlier hour in the evening than is now
customary, and might, if need be, close a little later. There
should be no difficulty in restricting the hours occupied by the
performance to four and a half.

To realise completely the motives of Hamlet's conduct, and the process of his fortunes, not a single utterance from the lips of the King, Polonius, or Laertes can be spared. In ordinary acting versions these three parts sink into insignificance. It is only in the full text that they assume their just and illuminating rank as Hamlet's foils.

The King rises into a character almost of the first class. He is a villain of unfathomable infamy, but his cowardly fear of the discovery of his crimes, his desperate pursuit of the consolations of religion, the quick ingenuity with which he plots escape from the inevitable retribution that dogs his misdeeds, excite —in the full text of the play—an interest hardly less intense than those wistful musings of the storm-tossed soul which stay his nephew's avenging hand.

Similarly, Hamlet's incisive wit and honesty are brought into the highest possible relief by the restoration to the feebly guileful Polonius of the speeches of which he has long been deprived. Among the reinstated scenes is that in which the meddlesome dotard teaches his servant Reynaldo modes of espionage that shall detect the moral lapses of his son Laertes in Paris. The recovered episode is not only admirable comedy, but it gives new vividness to Polonius's maudlin egotism which is responsible for many windings of the tragic plot.

The story is simplified at all points by such amplifications of the contracted version which holds the stage. The events are evolved with unsuspected naturalness. The hero's character gains by the expansion of its setting. One downright error which infects the standard abridgement is wholly avoided. Ophelia is dethroned. It is recognised that she is not entitled to share with Hamlet the triumphal honours of the action. Weak, insipid, destitute of all force of character, she deserves an insignificant place in Shakespeare's gallery of heroines. Hamlet's mother merits as much or more attention. At any rate, there is no justification for reducing the Queen's part in order to increase Ophelia's prominence. Such distortions are impossible in the production of the piece in its entirety. Throughout *Hamlet*, in the full authorised text, the artistic balance hangs true. Mr Benson recognised that dominant fact, and contrived to illustrate it on the stage. No higher commendation could be allowed a theatrical manager or actor.

IV

Much else could be said of Mr Benson's principles, and of his praiseworthy energy in seeking to familiarise the playgoer with Shakespearean drama in all its fulness and variety, but only one other specific feature of his method needs mention here. Perhaps the most convincing proof that he has given of the value of his principles to the country's dramatic art is his success in the training of actors and actresses. Of late it is his company that has supplied the great London actor-managers with their ablest recruits. Nearly all the best performers of secondary rôles and a few of the best performers of primary rôles in the leading London theatres are Mr Benson's pupils. Their admission to the great London companies is raising the standard of acting in the Metropolis. The marked efficiency of these newcomers is due to a system which is inconsistent with any of the accepted principles of current theatrical enterprise in London. Mr Benson's disciples mainly owe their efficiency to long association with a permanent company controlled by a manager who seeks, single-mindedly, what he holds to be the interests of dramatic art. The many-headed public learns its lessons very slowly, and sometimes neglects them altogether. It has been reluctant to recognise the true significance of Mr Benson's work. But the intelligent onlooker knows that he is marching along the right road, in intelligent conformity with the best teaching of the past.

Thirty years ago a meeting took place at the Mansion House to discuss the feasibility of founding a State theatre in London, a project which was not realised. The most memorable incident which was associated with the Mansion House meeting was a speech of the theatrical manager Phelps, who argued, amid the enthusiastic plaudits of his hearers, that it was in the highest interests of the nation that the Shakespearean drama should continuously occupy the stage. "I maintain," Phelps said, "from the experience of eighteen years, that the perpetual iteration of Shakespeare's words, if nothing more, going on daily for so many months of the year, must and would produce a great effect upon the public mind." No man or woman of sense will to-day gainsay the wisdom of this utterance; but it is needful for the public to make greater exertion than they have made of late if "the perpetual iteration of Shakespeare's words" in the theatre is to be permanently secured.

Mr Benson's efforts constitute the best organised endeavour to realise Phelps's ambition since Phelps

withdrew from management. Mr Benson's scheme
is imperfect in some of its details; in other particulars
it may need revision. But he and his associates
have planted their feet firmly on sure ground in their
endeavours to interpret Shakespearean drama constantly and in its variety, after a wise and well-
considered system and with a disinterested zeal.
When every allowance has been made for the Benson Company's shortcomings, its achievement cannot be denied "a relish of salvation." Mr Benson
deserves well of those who have faith in the power
of Shakespeare's words to widen the horizon of
men's intellects and emotions. The seed he has
sown should not be suffered to decay.

VI

THE MUNICIPAL THEATRE [1]

I

MANY actors, dramatic critics, and men in public life advocate the municipal manner of theatrical enterprise. Their aim, as I understand it, is to procure the erection, and the due working, of a playhouse that shall serve in permanence the best interests of the literary or artistic drama. The municipal theatre is not worth fighting for, unless there is a reasonable probability that its establishment will benefit dramatic art, promote the knowledge of dramatic literature, and draw from the literary drama and confer on the public the largest beneficial influence which the literary drama is capable of distributing.

None of Shakespeare's countrymen or countrywomen can deny with a good grace the importance of the drama as a branch of art. None will seriously dispute that our dramatic literature, at any rate in its loftiest manifestation, has contributed as much as our armies or our navies or our mechanical inventions to our reputation through the world.

There is substantial agreement among enlightened leaders of public opinion in all civilised coun-

[1] This paper was first printed in the *New Liberal Review,* May, 1902.

tries that great drama, when fitly represented in the theatre, offers the rank and file of a nation recreation which brings with it moral, intellectual, and spiritual advantage.

II

The first question to consider is whether in England the existing theatrical agencies promote for the general good the genuine interests of dramatic art. Do existing theatrical agencies secure for the nation all the beneficial influence that is derivable from the truly competent form of drama? If they do this sufficiently, it is otiose and impertinent to entertain the notion of creating any new theatrical agency.

Theatrical agencies of the existing type have never ignored the literary drama altogether. Among actor-managers of the past generation, Sir Henry Irving devoted his high ability to the interpretation of many species of literary drama—from that by Shakespeare to that by Tennyson. At leading theatres in London there have been produced in the last few years poetic dramas written in blank verse on themes drawn from such supreme examples of the world's · literature as Homer's *Odyssey* and Dante's *Inferno*. Signs have not been wanting of public anxiety to acknowledge with generosity these and other serious endeavours in poetic drama, whatever their precise degree of excellence. But such premisses warrant no very large conclusion. Two or three swallows do not make a summer. The literary drama is only welcomed to the London stage at uncertain intervals; most of its life is passed in the wilderness.

The recognition that is given in England to literary or poetic drama, alike of the past and present, is chiefly notable for its irregularity. The circumstance may be accounted for in various ways. It is best explained by the fact that England is the only country in Europe in which theatrical enterprise is wholly and exclusively organised on a capitalist basis. No theatre in England is worked to-day on any but the capitalist principle. Artistic aspiration may be well alive in the theatrical profession, but the custom and circumstance of capital, the calls of the counting-house, hamper the theatrical artist's freedom of action. The methods imposed are dictated too exclusively by the mercantile spirit.

Many illustrations could be given of the unceasing conflict which capitalist methods wage with artistic methods. One is sufficient. The commercially capitalised theatre is bound hand and foot to the system of long runs. In no theatres of the first class outside London and New York is the system known, and even here and in New York it is of comparatively recent origin. But Londoners have grown so accustomed to the system that they overlook the havoc which it works on the theatre as a home of art. Both actor and playgoer suffer signal injury from its effects. It limits the range of drama which is available at our great theatres to the rank and file of mankind. Especially serious is the danger to which the unchangeable programme exposes histrionic capacity and histrionic intelligence. The actor is not encouraged to widen his knowledge of the drama. His faculties are blunted by the narrow monotony of his experience. Yet the capitalised conditions of theatrical enterprise, which are in vogue in London and New York, seem to render long runs imperative. The system of long runs is peculiar to English-speaking countries, where alone theatrical enterprise is altogether under the sway of capital. It is specifically prohibited in the national or municipal theatre of every great foreign city, where the interests of dramatic art enjoy foremost consideration.

The artistic aspiration of the actor-manager may be set on the opposite side of the account. Although the actor-manager belongs to the ranks of the capitalists (whether he be one himself or dependent on one), yet when he exercises supreme control of his playhouse, and is moved by artistic feeling, he may check many of the evils that spring from capitalist domination. He can partially neutralise the hampering effect on dramatic art of the merely commercial application of capital to theatrical enterprise.

The actor-manager system is liable to impede the progress of dramatic art through defects of its own, but its most characteristic defects are not tarred with the capitalist brush. The actor-manager is prone to over-estimate the range of his histrionic power. He tends to claim of right the first place in the cast of every piece which he produces. He will consequently at times fill a rôle for which his powers unsuit him. If he be wise enough to avoid that error, he may imperil the interests of dramatic art in another fashion; he may neglect pieces, despite their artistic value, in which he knows the foremost part to be outside his scope. The actor-manager has sometimes undertaken a secondary rôle. But then it often happens, not necessarily by his deliberate endeavour, but by the mere force and popularity of his name among the frequenters of his playhouse, that there is focussed on his secondary part an attention that it does not intrinsically merit, with the result that the artistic perspective of the play is injured. A primary law of dramatic art deprecates the constant preponderance of one actor in a company. The highest attainable level of excellence in all the members is the true artistic aim.

The dangers inherent in the "star" principle of the actor-manager system may be frankly admitted, but at the same time one should recognise the system's possible advantages. An actor-manager does not usually arrive at his position until his career is well advanced and he has proved his histrionic capacity. Versatility commonly distinguishes him, and he is able to fill a long series of leading rôles without violating artistic propriety. At any rate, the actor-manager who resolutely cherishes respect for art can do much to temper the corrupting influences of commercial capitalism in the theatrical world.

It is probably the less needful to scrutinise closely the theoretic merits or demerits of the actor-manager system, because the dominant principle of current theatrical enterprise in London and America renders most precarious the future existence of that system. The actor-manager seems, at any rate, threatened in London by a new and irresistible tide of capitalist energy. Six or seven leading theatres in London have recently been brought under the control of an American capitalist who does not pretend to any but mercantile inspiration. The American capitalist's first and last aim is naturally to secure the highest possible remuneration for his

invested capital. He is catholic-minded, and has
no objection to artistic drama, provided he can
draw substantial profit from it. Material interests
alone have any real meaning for him. If he serve
the interests of art by producing an artistic play,
he serves art by accident and unconsciously: his
object is to benefit his exchequer. His philosophy
is unmitigated utilitarianism. "The greatest pleasure for the greatest number" is his motto. The
pleasure that carries farthest and brings round him
the largest paying audiences is his ideal stock-in-
trade. Obviously pleasure either of the frivolous or
of the spectacular kind attracts the greatest number
of customers to his emporium. It is consequently
pleasure of this spectacular or frivolous kind which
he habitually endeavours to provide. It is Quixotic
to anticipate much diminution in the supply and
demand of either frivolity or spectacle, both of
which may furnish quite innocuous pleasure. But
each is the antithesis of dramatic art; and whatever
view one holds of the methods of the American
capitalist, it is irrational to look to him for the intelligent promotion of dramatic art.

III

From the artistic point of view the modern
system of theatrical enterprise thus seems capable
of improvement. If it be incapable of general improvement, it is at least capable of having a better
example set it than current modes can be reckoned
on to offer. The latter are not likely to be dis-
placed. All that can be attempted is to create a
new model at their side. What is sought by the
advocates of a municipal theatre is an institution

which shall maintain in permanence a high artistic ideal of drama, and shall give the public the opportunity of permanently honouring that ideal. Existing theatres whose programmes ignore art would be unaffected by such a new neighbour. But existing enterprises, which, as far as present conditions permit, reflect artistic aspiration, would derive from such an institution new and steady encouragement.

The interests of dramatic art can only be served whole-heartedly in a theatre organised on two principles which have hitherto been unrecognised in England. In the first place, the management should acknowledge some sort of public obligation to make the interests of dramatic art its first motive of action. In the second place, the management should be relieved of the need of seeking unrestricted commercial profits for the capital that is invested in the venture. Both principles have been adopted with successful results in Continental cities; but their successful practice implies the acceptance by the State, or by a permanent local authority, of a certain amount of responsibility in both the artistic and the financial directions.

It is foolish to blind oneself to commercial considerations altogether. When the municipal theatre is freed of the unimaginative control of private capital seeking unlimited profit, it is still wise to require a moderate return on the expended outlay. The municipal theatre can only live healthily in the presence of a public desire or demand for it, and that public desire or demand can only be measured by the playhouse receipts. A municipal theatre would not be satisfactorily conducted if money were merely lost in it, or spent on it without any thought of the like-

lihood of the expenditure proving remunerative.
Profits need never be refused; but all above a fixed
minimum rate of interest on the invested capital
should be applied to the promotion of those purposes which the municipal theatre primarily exists
to serve—to cheapen, for example, prices of admission, or to improve the general mechanism behind
and before the scenes. No surplus profits should
reach the pocket of any individual manager or
financier.

IV

There is in England a demand and desire on the
part of a substantial section of the public for this
new form of theatrical enterprise, although its precise dimensions may not be absolutely determinable.
The question is thereby adapted for practical discussion. The demand and desire have as yet
received inadequate recognition, because they have
not been satisfactorily organised or concentrated.
The trend of an appreciable section of public opinion
in the direction of a limited municipalisation of
the theatre is visible in many places. Firstly, one
must take into account the number of small societies
which have been formed of late by enthusiasts for
the exclusive promotion of one or other specific
branch of the literary drama—the Elizabethan
drama, the Norwegian drama, the German drama.
Conspicuous success has been denied these societies
because their leaders tend to assert narrow sectional
views of the bases of dramatic art, or they lack the
preliminary training and the influence which are
essential to the efficient conduct of any public enterprise. Many of their experiences offer useful object-

lessons as to the defects inherent in all narrow sectional effort, however enthusiastically inspired.   But
at the same time they testify to a desire to introduce
into the current theatrical system more literary and
artistic principles than are at present habitual to
it.   They point to the presence of a zeal—often, it
may be, misdirected—for change or reform.

The experiment of Mr Benson points more
effectively in the same direction.   A public-spirited
champion of Shakespeare and the classical drama,
he has maintained his hold in the chief cities of
Ireland, Scotland, and the English provinces for a
generation.   Although for reasons that are not hard
to seek, he has failed to establish his position in
London, Mr Benson's methods of work have enabled him to render conspicuous service to the
London stage in a manner which is likely to facilitate
reform.   For many years he has supplied the leading London theatres with a succession of trained
actors and actresses.   Graduates in Mr Benson's
school can hardly fail to co-operate willingly in any
reform of theatrical enterprise, which is calculated
to develop the artistic capacities of the stage.

Other circumstances are no less promising.   The
justice of the cry for the due safeguarding of the
country's dramatic art by means of publicly-organ-
ised effort has been repeatedly acknowledged of late
by men of experience alike in dramatic and public
affairs.   In 1898 a petition was presented to the
London County Council requesting that body to
found and endow a permanent opera-house "in order
to promote the musical interest and refinement of
the public and the advancement of the art of music."
The petition bore the signatures of two hundred

leaders of public opinion, including the chief members of the dramatic profession. In this important document, particulars were given of the manner in which the State or the municipality aided theatres in France, Germany, Austria, and other countries of Europe. It was shown that in France twelve typically efficient theatres received from public bodies an annual subsidy amounting in the aggregate to £130,000.

The wording of the petition and the arguments employed by the petitioners were applicable to drama as well as to opera. In fact the case was put in a way which was more favourable to the pretensions of drama than to those of opera. One argument which always tells against the establishment of a publicly-subsidised opera-house in London does not affect the establishment of a publicly-subsidised theatre. Opera is an exotic in England; drama is a native product, and has exerted in the past a wider influence and has attracted a wider sympathy than Italian or German music.

The London County Council, after careful inquiry, gave the scheme of 1898 benevolent encouragement. Hope was held out that a site for either a theatre or an opera-house, might be reserved " in connection with one of the contemplated central improvements of London." Nothing in the recent history of the London County Council gives ground for doubting that it will be prepared to give practical effect to a thoroughly matured scheme.

Within the Council the principle of the municipal theatre has found powerful advocacy. Mr John Burns, who is not merely the spokesman of the working classes, but is a representative of earnest-

minded students of good literature, has supported
the principle with generous enthusiasm. The intelligent artisans of London applaud his attitude.
The London Trades Council passed resolutions in
the autumn of 1901 recommending the erection of a
theatre by the London County Council, "so that a
higher standard of dramatic art might be encouraged
and made more accessible to the wage-earning classes
as is the case in the State and municipal theatres
in the principal cities on the Continent." The gist
of the argument could hardly be put more plainly.

Of those who have written recently in favour of
the scheme of a municipal theatre many speak with
the authority of exceptional experience. The actor
Mr John Coleman, one of the last survivors of
Phelps's company at Sadler's Wells Theatre, argued
with cogency, shortly before his death in 1903, that
the national credit owed it to itself to renew Phelps's
experiment of the middle of last century; public
intervention was imperative, seeing that no other
means were forthcoming. The late Sir Henry Irving
in his closing years announced his conviction that
a municipal theatre could alone keep the classical
and the poetic drama fully alive in the theatres.
The dramatic critic, Mr William Archer, has brought
his expert knowledge of dramatic organisation at
home and abroad to the aid of the agitation. Various proposals — unhappily of too vague and un-
authoritative a kind to guarantee a satisfactory
reception—have been made from time to time to
raise a fund to build a national theatre, and to run it
for five years on a public subsidy of £10,000 a year.

The advocates of the municipalising principle
have worked for the most part in isolation. Such

independence tends to dissipate rather than to conserve energy. A consolidating impulse has been sorely needed. But the variety of the points of views from which the subject has been independently approached renders the less disputable the genuine width of public interest in the question.

The argument that it is contrary to public policy, or that it is opposed to the duty of the State or municipality, to provide for the people's enlightened amusement, is not formidable. The State and the municipality have long treated such work as part of their daily functions, whatever the arguments that have been urged against it. The State, in partnership with local authorities, educates the people, whether they like it or no. The municipalities of London and other great towns provide the people, outside the theatre, with almost every opportunity of enlightenment and enlightened amusement. In London there are 150 free libraries, which are mainly occupied in providing the ratepayers with the opportunities of reading fiction—recreation which is not always very enlightened. The County Council of London furnishes bands of music to play in the parks, at an expenditure of some £6000 a year. Most of our great cities supply, in addition, municipal picture galleries, in which the citizens take pride, and to which in their corporate capacity they contribute large sums of money. The municipal theatre is the natural complement of the municipal library, the municipal musical entertainment, and the municipal art gallery.

V

Of the practicability of a municipal theatre ample evidence is at hand. Foreign experience convincingly justifies the municipal mode of theatrical enterprise. Every great town in France, Germany, Austria, and Switzerland has its municipal theatre. In Paris there are three, in addition to four theatres which are subsidised by the State. It is estimated that there are seventy municipal theatres in the German-speaking countries of Europe, apart from twenty-seven State theatres. At the same time, it should be noted that in the French and German capitals there are, at the side of the State and municipal playhouses, numerous theatres which are run on ordinary commercial lines. The prosperity of these houses is in no way checked by the contiguity of theatrical enterprise of State or municipality.

All municipal theatres on the continent of Europe pursue the same aims. They strive to supply the citizens with true artistic drama continuously, and to reduce the cost of admission to the playhouse to the lowest possible terms. But the working details of the foreign municipal theatres differ widely in individual cases, and a municipality which contemplates a first theatrical experiment is offered a large choice of method. In some places the municipality acts with regal munificence, and directly assumes the largest possible responsibilities. It provides the site, erects the theatre, and allots a substantial subsidy to its maintenance. The manager is a municipal officer, and the municipal theatre fills in the social life of the town as imposing a place as the town-hall, cathedral, or university.

Elsewhere the municipality sets narrower limits to its sphere of operations. It merely provides the site and the building, and then lets the playhouse out at a moderate rental to directors of proved efficiency and public spirit, on assured conditions that they honestly serve the true interests of art, uphold a high standard of production, avoid the frivolity and spectacle of the market, and fix the price of seats on a very low scale. Here no public funds are seriously involved. The municipality pays no subsidy. The rent of the theatre supplies the municipality with normal interest on the capital that is invested in site and building. It is public credit of a moral rather than of a material kind which is pledged to the cause of dramatic art.

In a third class of municipal theatre the public body confines its material aid to the gratuitous provision of a site. Upon that site private enterprise is invited to erect a theatre under adequate guarantee that it shall exclusively respect the purposes of art, and spare to the utmost the pockets of the playgoer. To render dramatic art accessible to the rank and file of mankind, with the smallest possible pressure on the individual citizen's private resources, is of the essence of every form of municipal theatrical enterprise.

The net result of the municipal theatre, especially in German-speaking countries, is that the literary drama, both of the past and present, maintains a grip on the playgoing public which is outside English experience. There is in Germany a very flourishing modern German drama of literary merit. Sudermann and Hauptmann hold the ears of men of letters throughout Europe. Dramas by these authors

are constantly presented in municipal theatres.
At the same time, plays by the classical dramatists
of all European countries are performed as constantly, and are no less popular. Almost every play
of Shakespeare is in the repertory of the chief
acting companies on the German municipal stage.
At the side of Shakespeare stand Schiller and Goethe
and Lessing, the classical dramatists of Germany;
Molière, the classical dramatist of France; and
Calderon, the classical dramatist of Spain. Public
interest is liberally distributed over the whole range
of artistic dramatic effort. Indeed, during recent
years, Shakespeare's plays have been performed in
Germany more often than plays of the modern German school. Schiller, the classical national dramatist of Germany, lives more conspicuously on the
modern German stage than any one modern German
contemporary writer, eminent and popular as more
than one contemporary German dramatist deserved-
ly is. Thus signally has the national or municipal
system of theatrical enterprise in Germany served
the cause of classical drama. All the beneficial influence and gratification, which are inherent in artistic and literary drama, are, under the national
or municipal system, enjoyed in permanence and
security by the German people.

Vienna probably offers London the most in-
structive example of the national or municipal
theatre. The three leading Viennese playhouses—
the Burg-Theater, the Stadt-Theater, and the Volks-
Theater—illustrate the three modes in which public
credit may be pledged to theatrical enterprise. The
palatial Burg-Theater is wholly an institution of the
State. The site of the Stadt-Theater, and to a

large extent the building, were provided by the municipality, which thereupon leased them out to a private syndicate, under a manager of the syndicate's choosing. The municipality assumes no more direct responsibility for the due devotion of the Stadt-Theater to dramatic art than is implied in its retention of reversionary rights of ownership. The third theatre, the Volks-Theater, illustrates the minimum share that a municipality may take in promoting theatrical enterprise, while guaranteeing the welfare of artistic drama.

The success of the Volks-Theater is due to the co-operation of a public body with a voluntary society of private citizens who regard the maintenance of the literary drama as a civic duty. The site of the Volks-Theater, which was formerly public property and estimated to be worth £80,000, is in the best part of the city of Vienna. It was a free gift from the government to a limited liability company, formed of some four hundred shareholders of moderate means, who formally pledged themselves to erect on the land a theatre with the sole object of serving the purposes of dramatic art. The interest payable to shareholders is strictly limited by the conditions of association. An officially sanctioned constitution renders it obligatory on them and on their officers to produce in the playhouse classical and modern drama of a literary character, though not necessarily of the severest type. Merely frivolous or spectacular pieces are prohibited, and at least twice a week purely classical plays must be presented. No piece may be played more than two nights in immediate succession. The actors, whose engagements are permanent, are substantially paid, and an admirably devised system of pensions is enforced without making deductions from salaries. The price of seats is fixed at a low rate, the highest price being 4s., the cheapest and most numerous seats costing 10d. each. Both financially and artistically the result has been all that one could wish. There is no public subsidy, but the Emperor pays £500 a year for a box. The house holds 1800 persons, yielding gross receipts of £200 for a nightly expenditure of £125. There are no advertising expenses, no posters. The newspapers give notice of the daily programme as an attractive item of news.

VI

There is some disinclination among Englishmen deliberately to adopt foreign methods, to follow foreign examples, in any walk of life. But no person of common sense will reject a method merely because it is foreign, if it can be proved to be of utility. It is spurious patriotism to reject wise counsel because it is no native product. On the other hand, it is seriously to asperse the culture and intelligence of the British nation to assume that no appreciable section of it cherishes that taste for the literary drama which keeps the national or municipal theatre alive in France and Germany. At any rate, judgment should be held in suspense until the British playgoers' mettle has been more thoroughly tested than hitherto.

No less humiliating is the argument that the art of acting in this country is at too low an ebb to justify the assumption by a public body of responsibility for theatrical enterprise. One or two critics assert that to involve public credit in a theatre, until there exist an efficient school of acting, is to put the cart before the horse. This objection seems insubstantial. Competent actors are not altogether absent from the English stage, and the municipal system of theatrical enterprise is calculated to increase their number rapidly.

Abroad, the subsidised theatres, with their just schemes of salary, their permanent engagements, their well-devised pension systems, attract the best class of the profession. A competent company of actors, which enjoys a permanent home and is governed by high standards of art, forms the best possible school of acting, not merely by force of example, but by the private tuition which it could readily provide. In Vienna the companies at the subsidised theatres are recruited from the pupils of a State-endowed conservatoire of actors. It is improbable that the British Government will found a like institution. But it would be easy to attach a college of acting to the municipal theatre, and to make the college pay its way.

Much depends on the choice of manager of the enterprise. The manager of a municipal theatre must combine with business aptitude a genuine devotion to dramatic art and dramatic literature. Without a fit manager, who can collect and control a competent company of actors, the scheme of the municipal theatre is doomed to failure. Managers of the requisite temper, knowledge, and ability are not lacking in France or Germany. There is no reason to anticipate that, when the call is sounded, the right response will not be given here.

Cannot an experiment be made in London on

the lines of the Vienna Volks-Theater?   In the first
place, it is needful to bring together a body of citizens
who, under leadership which commands public confidence, will undertake to build and control for a
certain term of years a theatre of suitable design
in the interests of dramatic art, on conditions similar to those that have worked with success in Berlin, Paris, and notably Vienna.   Then the London
County Council after the professions it has made,
might be reasonably expected to undertake so much
responsibility for the proper conduct of the new
playhouse as would be implied by its provision of
a site.   If the experiment failed, no one would be
much the worse; if it succeeded, as it ought to suc-
ceed, the nation would gain in repute for intelligence,
culture, and enlightened patriotism; it would rid
itself of the reproach that it pays smaller and less
intelligent regard to Shakespeare and the literary
drama than France, Germany, Austria, or Italy.

Phelps's single-handed effort brought the people
of London for eighteen years face to face with the
great English drama at his playhouse at Sadler's
Wells.   "I made that enterprise pay," he said, after
he retired; "not making a fortune certainly, but
bringing up a large family and paying my way."
Private troubles and illness compelled him suddenly
to abandon the enterprise at the end of eighteen
years, when there happened to be none at hand to
take his place of leader.   All that was wanting to
make his enterprise permanent, he declared, was
some public control, some public acknowledgment of
responsibility which, without impeding the efficient
manager's freedom of action, would cause his post to
be properly filled in case of an accidental vacancy.

Phelps thought that if he could do so much during eighteen years by his personal, isolated, and independent endeavour, much more could be done in permanence under some public method of safeguard and guarantee. Phelps's services to the literary drama can hardly be over-estimated. His mature judgment is not to be lightly gainsaid. It is just to his memory to put his faith to a practical test.

VII

ASPECTS OF SHAKESPEARE'S PHILOSOPHY [1]

I

A FRENCH critic once remarked that a whole system of philosophy could be deduced from Shakespeare's pages, though from all the works of the philosophers one could not draw a page of Shakespeare. The second statement—the denial of the presence of a page of Shakespeare in the works of all the philosophers—is more accurate than the assertion that a system of philosophy could be deduced from the plays of Shakespeare. It is hopeless to deduce any precise system of philosophy from Shakespeare's plays. Literally, philosophy means nothing more recondite than love of wisdom. Technically, it means scientifically restrained speculation about the causes of human thought and conduct; it embraces the sciences of logic, of ethics, of politics, of psychology, of metaphysics. Shakespeare's training and temper unfitted him to make any professed contribution to any of these topics.

Ignorant persons argue on hazy grounds that the great avowed philosopher of Shakespeare's day,

[1] This paper, which was originally prepared in 1899 for the purposes of a popular lecture, is here printed for the first time.

142

Francis Bacon, wrote Shakespeare's plays.   There is
no need to confute the theory, which confutes itself.
But, if a confutation were needed, it lies on the sur-
face in the conflicting attitudes which Shakespeare
and Bacon assume towards philosophy.   There is
no mistaking Bacon's attitude.   The supreme aim
of his writings was to establish the practical value,
the majestic importance, of philosophy in its strict
sense of speculative science.   He sought to widen
its scope and to multiply the ranks of its students.

Bacon's method is formally philosophic in texture.
He carefully scrutinises, illustrates, seeks to justify
each statement before proceeding to a conclusion.
Every essay, every treatise of Bacon, conveys the impression not merely of weighty, pregnant eloquence,
but of the argumentative and philosophic temper.
Bacon's process of thinking is conscious: it is visible
behind the words.   The argument progresses with
a cumulative force.   It draws sustenance from the
recorded opinions of others.   The points usually
owe consistency and firmness to quotations from old
authors—Greek and Latin authors, especially Plató
and Plutarch, Lucretius and Seneca.   To Bacon, as
to all professed students of the subject, philosophy
first revealed itself in the pages of the Greek writers
Plato and Aristotle, the founders for modern Europe
of the speculative sciences of human thought and
conduct.   Greatly as Bacon modified the Greek
system of philosophy, he began his philosophic career
under the influence of Aristotle, and, despite his de-
structive criticism of his master, he never wholly
divested himself of the methods of exposition to
which the Greek philosopher's teaching introduced
him.

In their attitudes to philosophy, Shakespeare and Bacon are as the poles asunder. Shakespeare practically ignores the existence of philosophy as a formal science. He betrays no knowledge of its Greek origin and developments.

There are two short, slight, conventional mentions of Aristotle's name in Shakespeare's works. One is a very slight allusion to Aristotle's "checks" or "moral discipline" in *The Taming of the Shrew*. That passage is probably from a coadjutor's pen. In any case it is merely a playful questioning of the title of "sweet philosophy" to monopolize a young man's education.[1]

The other mention of Aristotle is in *Troilus and Cressida*, and raises points of greater interest. Hector scornfully likens his brothers Troilus and Paris, when they urge persistence in the strife with Greece, to "young men whom Aristotle thought unfit to hear *moral* philosophy" (II. 2, 166). The words present the meaning, but not the language, of a sentence in Aristotle's "Nicomachean Ethics" (i. 8). Aristotle there declares passionate youth to be unfitted to study *political* philosophy; he makes no mention of *moral* philosophy. The change of epithet does, however, no injustice to Aristotle's argument. His context makes it plain, that by

[1] Tranio, the attendant on the young Pisan, Lucentio, who has come to Padua to study at the university, counsels his master to widen the field of his studies:—

> Only, good master, while we do admire
> This virtue and this moral discipline,
> Let's be no Stoics, nor no stocks, I pray,
> Or so devote to *Aristotle's checks*,
> As Ovid be an outcast quite adjured.
> —*The Taming of the Shrew*, i. 2, 29–33.

political philosophy he means the ethics of civil
society, which are hardly distinguishable from what
is commonly called "morals." The maxim, in the
slightly irregular shape which Shakespeare adopted,
enjoyed proverbial currency before the dramatist
was born. Erasmus introduced it in this form into
his far-famed *Colloquies*. In France and Italy the
warning against instructing youth in *moral* philosophy was popularly accepted as an Aristotelian in-
junction. Sceptics about the obvious Shakespearean
tradition have made much of the circumstance that
Bacon, who cited the aphorism from Aristotle in his
Advancement of Learning, substituted, like Shakespeare in *Troilus and Cressida*, the epithet "moral"
for "political." The proverbial currency of the
emendation deprives the coincidence of point.

The repetition of a proverbial phrase, indirectly
drawn from Aristotle, combined with the absence of
other references to the Greek philosopher, renders
improbable Shakespeare's personal acquaintance
with his work. In any case, the bare mention of
the name of Aristotle implies nothing in this connection. It was a popular synonym for ancient
learning. It was as often on the lips of Elizabethans
as Bacon's name is on the lips of men and women of
to-day, and it would be rash to infer that those who
carelessly and casually mentioned Bacon's name to-
day knew Bacon's writings or philosophic theories
at first hand.

No evidence is forthcoming that Shakespeare
knew in any solid sense aught of philosophy of the
formal scientific kind. On scientific philosophy, and
on natural science, Shakespeare probably looked
with suspicion. He expressed no high opinion of

astronomers, who pursue the most imposing of all branches of scientific speculation.

> Small have continual plodders ever won,
> Save base authority from others' books.
> These earthly godfathers of heaven's light,
> That give a name to every fixed star,
> Have no more profit of their shining nights
> Than those that walk, and wot not what they are.
> —*Love's Labour's Lost*, I., i., 86–91.

This is a characteristically poetic attitude; it is the antithesis of the scientific attitude. Formal logic excited Shakespeare's disdain even more conspicuously. In the mouths of his professional fools he places many reductions to absurdity of what he calls the "simple syllogism." He invests the term "chop-logic" with the significance of foolery *in excelsis*.[1] Again, metaphysics, in any formal sense, were clearly not of Shakespeare's world. On one occasion he wrote of the topic round which most metaphysical speculation revolves:—

> We are such stuff
> As dreams are made on, and our little life
> Is rounded by a sleep.
> —*The Tempest*, IV., i., 156–8.

---

[1] The speeches of the clown in *Twelfth Night* are particularly worthy of study for the satiric adroitness with which they expose the quibbling futility of syllogistic logic. *Cf.* Act I., Scene V., ll. 43–57:

Olivia. Go to, you're a dry fool; I'll no more of you: besides you grow dishonest.

Clown. Two faults, Madonna, that drink and good counsel will amend: for give the dry fool drink, then is the fool not dry: bid the dishonest man mend himself; if he mend, he is no longer dishonest; if he cannot, let the botcher mend him. Anything that's mended is but patched: virtue that transgresses is but patched with sin; and sin that amends is but patched with virtue. If that *this simple syllogism* will serve, so; if it will not, what remedy?

Such a theory of human life is first-rate poetry; it is an illuminating figure of poetic speech. But the simplicity with which the theme is presented, to the exclusion of many material issues, puts the statement out of the plane of metaphysical disquisition, which involves subtle conflict of argument and measured resolution of doubt, rather than imaginative certainty or unconditional assertion. Nor is Hamlet's famous soliloquy on the merits and demerits of suicide conceived in the spirit of the metaphysician. It is a dramatic description of a familiar phase of emotional depression; it explains nothing; it propounds no theory. It reflects a state of feeling; it breathes that torturing spirit of despondency which kills all hope of mitigating either the known ills of life or the imagined terrors of death.

The faint, shadowy glimpses which Shakespeare had of scientific philosophy gave him small respect for it. Like the typical hard-headed Englishman, he doubted its practical efficacy. Shakespeare viewed all formal philosophy much as Dr Johnson's Rasselas, whose faith in it dwindled, when he perceived that the professional philosopher, who preached superiority to all human frailties and weaknesses, succumbed to them at the first provocation.

> There are more things in heaven and earth
> Than are dreamt of in your philosophy.[1]

> For there was never yet philosopher
> That could endure the toothache patiently.[2]

---

[1] *Hamlet*, I., v., 166–7.
[2] *Much Ado About Nothing*, V., i., 35–6.

Such phrases sum up Shakespeare's habitual bearing to formal philosophy. The consideration of causes, first principles, abstract truths never, in the dramatist's opinion, cured a human ill. The futility of formal philosophy stands, from this point of view, in no further need of demonstration.

II

But it is permissible to use the words philosopher and philosophy, without scientific precision or significance, in the popular inaccurate senses of shrewd observer and observation of life. By philosophy we may understand common-sense wisdom about one's fellow-men, their aspirations, their failures and successes. As soon as we employ the word in that significance, we must allow that few men were better philosophers than Shakespeare.

Shakespeare is what Touchstone calls the shepherd in *As You Like It*—"a natural philosopher" —an observer by light of nature, an acute expositor of phases of human life and feeling. Character, thought, passion, emotion, form the raw material of which ethical or metaphysical systems are made. The poet's contempt for formal ethical or metaphysical theory co-existed with a searching knowledge of the ultimate foundations of all systematised philosophic structures. The range of fact or knowledge within which the formal theorist speculates in the fields of ethics, logic, metaphysics, or psychology, is, indeed, very circumscribed when it is compared with the region of observation and experience, over which Shakespeare exerted complete mastery.

Almost every aspect of life Shakespeare portrays

with singular evenness of insight. He saw life whole. The web of life always presented itself to him as a mingled yarn, good and ill together. He did not stay to reconcile its contradictions. He adduces a wealth of evidence touching ethical experience. It may be that the patient scrutiny of formal philosophers can alone reveal the full significance of his harvest. But the dramatist's exposition of the workings of virtue or vice have no recondite intention. Shakespeare was no patient scholar, who deliberately sought to extend the limits of human knowledge. With unrivalled ease and celerity he digested, in the recesses of his consciousness, the fruit of personal observation and reading. His aim was to depict only conscious human conduct and human thought. He interpreted them unconsciously, by virtue of an involuntary intuition.

Shakespeare's intuition pierces life at the lowest as well as at the highest level of experience. It is coloured by delicate imaginative genius as well as by robust and practical worldliness. Not his writings only, but the facts of his private life—his mode of managing his private property, for example—attest his alert knowledge of the material and practical affairs of human existence. Idealism and realism in perfect development were interwoven with the texture of his mind.

Shakespeare was qualified by mental endowment for success in any career. He was by election a dramatist and, necessarily, one of unmatched versatility. His intuitive faculty enabled him, after regarding life from any point of view that he willed, to depict through the mouths of his characters the chosen phase of life in convincing, harmonious accord with his characters' individual circumstances and experiences. No obvious trace of his own personal circumstance or experience was suffered to emerge in the utterances of his characters, who lived for the moment in his brain. It is a commonplace to credit Shakespeare with supreme dramatic instinct. It is difficult fully to realise the significance of that attribute. It means that he could contract or expand at will and momentarily his own personality, so that it coincided exactly, now with a self-indulgent humorist like Falstaff, now with an introspective student like Hamlet, now with a cynical criminal like Iago, now with a high-spirited girl like Rosalind, now with an ambitious woman like Lady Macbeth, and then with a hundred more characters hardly less distinctive than these. It means that he could contrive the coincidence so absolutely as to leave no loophole for the introduction, into the several dramatic utterances, of any sentiment that should not be on the face of it adapted by right of nature to the speaker's idiosyncrasies. That was Shakespeare's power. It is a power of which the effects are far easier to recognise than the causes or secret of operation.

In the present connection it is happily only necessary to dwell on Shakespeare's dramatic instinct in order to guard against the peril of dogmatising from his works about his private opinions. So various and conflicting are Shakespeare's dramatic pronouncements on phases of experience that it is difficult and dangerous to affirm which pronouncements, if any, present most closely his personal sentiment. He fitted the lips of his *dramatis personæ* with speeches and sentiments so peculiarly adapted to them as to show no one quite undisputed sign of their creator's personality.

Yet there are occasions when, without detracting from the omnipotence of Shakespeare's dramatic instinct, one may tentatively infer that Shakespeare gave voice through his created personages to sentiments which were his own. The Shakespearean drama must incorporate somewhere within its vast limits the personal thoughts and passions of its creator, even although they are for the most part absorbed past recognition in the mighty mass, and no critical chemistry can with confidence disentangle them. At any rate, there are in the plays many utterances—ethical utterances, or observations conceived in the spirit of "a natural philosopher"— which are repeated to much the same effect at different periods of the poet's career. These reiterated opinions frequently touch the conditions of well-being or calamity in civilised society; they often deal with man in civic or social relation with his neighbour; they define the capabilities of his will. It is unlikely that observations of this nature would be repeated if the sentiments they embody were out of harmony with the author's private conviction. Often we shall not strain a point or do our critical sense much violence if we assume that these recurring thoughts are Shakespeare's own. I purpose to call attention to a few of those which bear on large questions of government and citizenship and human volition. Involuntarily, they form the framework of a political and moral philosophy, which for clear-eyed sanity is without rival.

III

Shakespeare's political philosophy is instinct with the loftiest moral sense. Directly or indirectly, he defines many times the essential virtues and the inevitable temptations which attach to persons exercising legalised authority over their fellow-men. The topic always seems to stir in Shakespeare his most serious tone of thought and word. No one, in fact, has conceived a higher standard of public virtue and public duty than Shakespeare. His intuition rendered him tolerant of human imperfection. He is always in kindly sympathy with failure, with suffering, with the oppressed. Consequently he brings at the outset into clearer relief than professed political philosophers, the saving quality of mercy in rulers of men. Twice Shakespeare pleads in almost identical terms, through the mouths of created characters, for generosity on the part of governors of states towards those who sin against law. In both cases he places his argument, with significant delicacy, on the lips of women. At a comparatively early period in his career as dramatist, in *The Merchant of Venice*, Portia first gave voice to the political virtue of compassion. At a much later period Shakespeare set the same plea in the mouth of Isabella in *Measure for Measure*. The passages are too familiar to justify quotation. Very brief extracts will bring out clearly the identity of sentiment which finds definition in the two passages.

These are Portia's views of mercy on the throne (*Merchant of Venice*, IV., i., 188 *seq.*):—

'Tis mightiest in the mightiest; it becomes
The throned monarch better than his crown;

. . . . . .

> Mercy is above this sceptred sway;
> It is enthroned in the hearts of kings,
> It is an attribute to God himself;
> And earthly power doth then show likest God's,
> When mercy seasons justice.

> Consider this,
> That in the course of justice none of us
> Should see salvation.[1]

Here are Isabella's words in *Measure for Measure* (II., ii., 59 *seq.*):—

> No ceremony that to great ones 'longs,
> Not the king's crown, nor the deputed sword,
> The marshal's truncheon, nor the judge's robe,
> Become them with one half so good a grace
> As mercy does.

> How would you be
> If He, which is the top of judgment, should
> But judge you as you are?

> O, it is excellent
> To have a giant's strength; but it is tyrannous
> To use it like a giant.

Mercy is the predominating or crowning virtue that Shakespeare demands in rulers. But the Shakespearean code is innocent of any taint of

---

[1] In a paper on " Latin as an Intellectual Force," read before the International Congress of Arts and Sciences at St. Louis in September, 1904, Professor E. A. Sonnenschein sought to show that Portia's speech on mercy is based on Seneca's tract, *De Clementia*. The most striking parallel passages are the following:—

> It becomes
> The throned monarch better than his crown. (*M. of V.*, IV., i., 189–90.)

Nullum clementia ex omnibus magis quam regem aut principem decet. (Seneca, *De Clementia*, I., iii., 3.):—

> 'Tis mightiest in the mightiest.

sentimentality, and mercifulness is far from being the sovereign's sole qualification or primal test of fitness.   More especially are kings and judges bound by their responsibilities and their duties to eschew self-glorification or self-indulgence.   It is the *virtues* of the holders of office, not their office itself, which entitles them to consideration.   Adventitious circumstances give no man claim to respect.   A man is alone worthy of regard by reason of his personal character.   Honour comes from his own acts, neither from his "foregoers" (*i.e.*, ancestors) nor from his

Eo scilicet formosius id esse magnificentiusque fatebimur quo in maiore praestabitur potestate (I., xix., 1):—

> But mercy is above this sceptred sway,
> It is enthroned in the hearts of kings:
> It is an attribute of God Himself.
>   —*M. of V.*, IV., i., *193–5.*

Quod si di placabiles et aequi delicta potentium non statim fulminibus persequuntur, quanto aequius est hominem hominibus praepositum miti animo exercere imperium? (I., vii., 2):—

> And earthly power doth then show likest God's
> When mercy seasons justice.
>   —*M. of V.*, IV., i., *196–7.*

Quid autem?   Non proximum eis (dis) locum tenet is qui se ex deorum natura gerit beneficus et largus et in melius potens? (I., xix., 9):—

> Consider this,
> That, in the course of justice, none of us
> Should see salvation.
>   —*M. of V.*, IV., i., *198–200.*

Cogitato . . . quanta solitudo et vastitas futura sit si nihil relinquitur nisi quod iudex severus absolverit (I., vi., 1).

This remarkable series of parallelisms does not affect the argument in the text that Shakespeare, who reiterated Portia's pleas in similar phraseology in Isabella's speeches, had a personal faith in the declared sentiment.   Whether the parallelism is to be explained as conscious borrowing or accidental coincidence is an open question.

rank in society. "Good alone is good without a name." This is not the view of the world, which values lying trophies, rank, or wealth. The world is thereby the sufferer.[1]

The world honours a judge; but if the judge be indebted to his office and not to his character for the respect that is paid him, he may deserve no more honour than the criminal in the dock, whom he sentences to punishment. "A man may see how this world goes with no eyes," says King Lear to the blind Gloucester. "Look with thine ears; see how yond justice rails upon yond simple thief. Hark, in thine ear; change places, and, handy-dandy, which is the justice, which is the thief? Thou hast seen a farmer's dog bark at a beggar? And the creature run from the cur? There thou mightst behold the great image of authority; a dog's obeyed in office." "The great image of authority" is often a brazen idol.

Hereditary rulers form no inconsiderable section of Shakespeare's *dramatis personæ*. In *Macbeth* (IV.,

[1] From lowest place, when virtuous things proceed,
  The place is dignified by the doer's deed:
  Where great additions swell 's, and virtue none,
  It is a dropsied honour: good alone
  Is good without a name; vileness is so:
  The property by what it is should go,
  Not by the title; . . . that is honour's scorn,
  Which challenges itself as honour's born,
  And is not like the sire: honours thrive
  When rather from our acts we them derive
  Than our foregoers: the mere word 's a slave,
  Debauch'd on every tomb; on every grave
  A lying trophy; and as oft is dumb
  Where dust and damn'd oblivion is the tomb
  Of honour'd bones indeed.
        —*All's Well*, II., iii., 130 *seq.*

iii., 92–4) he specifically defined "the king-becoming graces":—

> As justice, verity, temperance, stableness,
> Bounty, perseverance, mercy, lowliness,
> Devotion, patience, courage, fortitude.

But the dramatist's main energies are devoted to exposure of the hollowness of this counsel of perfection. Temptations to vice beset rulers of men to a degree that is unknown to their subjects. To avarice rulers are especially prone. Stanchless avarice constantly converts kings of ordinary clay into monsters. How often they forge

> Quarrels unjust against the good and loyal,
> Destroying them for wealth.
>> —*Macbeth,* IV., iii., 83–4.

Intemperance in all things—in work and pleasure —is a standing menace of monarchs.

> Boundless intemperance
> In Nature is a tyranny: it hath been
> Th' untimely emptying of the happy throne
> And fall of many kings.
>> —*Macbeth,* IV., iii., 66–9.

A leader of men, if he be capable of salvation, must "delight no less in truth than life." Yet "truth," for the most part, is banished from the conventional environment of royalty.

Repeatedly does Shakespeare bring into dazzling relief the irony which governs the being of kings. Want of logic and defiance of ethical principle underlie their pride in magnificent ceremonial and pageantry. The ironic contrast between the pretensions of a king and the actual limits of human destiny is a text which Shakespeare repeatedly clothes in golden language.

It is to be admitted that nearly all the kings in

Shakespeare's gallery frankly acknowledge the make-believe and unreality which dogs regal pomp and ceremony. In self-communion they acknowledge the ruler's difficulty in finding truth in their traditional scope of life. In a great outburst on the night before Agincourt, Henry V.—the only king whom Shakespeare seems thoroughly to admire—openly describes the inevitable confusion between fact and fiction which infects the conditions of royalty. Anxiety and unhappiness are so entwined with ceremonial display as to deprive the king of the reliefs and recreations which freely lie at the disposal of ordinary men.

> What infinite heart's-ease
> Must kings neglect that private men enjoy!
> And what have kings that privates have not too,
> Save ceremony, save general ceremony?
> And what art thou, thou idol ceremony?
> What kind of god art thou, that suffer'st more
> Of mortal griefs than do thy worshippers?
> What are thy rents? what are thy comings-in?
> O ceremony, show me but thy worth!
> What is thy soul of adoration?
> Art thou aught else but place, degree, and form,
> Creating awe and fear in other men?
> Wherein thou art less happy being fear'd
> Than they in fearing.
> What drink'st thou oft, instead of homage sweet,
> But poison'd flattery? O, be sick, great greatness,
> And bid thy ceremony give thee cure!
> Think'st thou the fiery fever will go out
> With titles blown from adulation?
> Will it give place to flexure and low bending?
> Canst thou, when thou command'st the beggar's knee,
> Command the health of it?   No, thou proud dream
> That play'st so subtly with a king's repose:
> I am a king that find thee; and I know
> 'Tis not the balm, the sceptre, and the ball,
> The sword, the mace, the crown imperial,
> The intertissued robe of gold and pearl,

> The farced title running 'fore the king,
> The throne he sits on, nor the tide of pomp
> That beats upon the high shore of this world,—
> No, not all these, thrice gorgeous ceremony,
> Not all these, laid in bed majestical,
> Can sleep so soundly as the wretched slave
> Who, with a body fill'd and vacant mind
> Gets him to rest, cramm'd with distressful bread.
> —*Henry V.*, IV., i., 253–87.

Barely distinguishable is the sentiment which finds expression in the pathetic speech of Henry V.'s father when he vainly seeks that sleep which thousands of his poorest subjects enjoy. The sleepless king points to the irony of reclining on the kingly couch beneath canopies of costly state when sleep refuses to weigh his eyelids down or steep his senses in forgetfulness. The king is credited with control of every comfort; but he is denied by nature comforts which she places freely at command of the humblest. So again does Richard II. soliloquize on the vain pride which imbues the king, while death all the time grins at his pomp and keeps his own court within the hollow crown that rounds the prince's mortal temples. Yet again, to identical effect is Henry VI.'s sorrowful question:

> Gives not the hawthorn-bush a sweeter shade,
> To shepherds looking on their silly sheep,
> Than doth a rich-embroidered canopy
> To kings that fear their subjects' treachery?
> —*3 Henry VI.*, II., v., 42–5.

To this text Shakespeare constantly recurs, and he bestows on it all his fertile resources of illustration. The reiterated exposition by Shakespeare of the hollowness of kingly ceremony is a notable feature of his political sentiment. The dramatist's independent analysis of the quiddity of kingship is, in-

deed, alike in manner and matter, a startling contribution to sixteenth century speculation.   In manner it is worthy of Shakespeare's genius at its
highest.   In matter it is for its day revolution-
ary rationalism.   It defies a popular doctrine, held
almost universally by Shakespeare's contemporary
fellow-countrymen, that royalty is divine and under
God's special protection, that the gorgeous ceremony
of the throne reflects a heavenly attribute, and that
the king is the pampered favourite of heaven.

Bacon defined a king with slender qualifications,
as "a mortal god on earth unto whom the living God
has lent his own name."   Shakespeare was well
acquainted with this accepted doctrine.   He often
gives dramatic definition of it.   He declines to admit
its soundness.   Wherever he quotes it, he adds an
ironical comment, which was calculated to perturb
the orthodox royalist.   Having argued that the
day-labourer or the shepherd is far happier than a
king, he logically refuses to admit that the monarch
is protected by God from any of the ills of mortality.
Richard II. may assert that "the hand of God alone,
and no hand of blood or bone" can rob him of the
sacred handle of his sceptre.   But the catastrophe
of the play demonstrates that that theft is entirely
within human scope.   The king is barbarously murdered.   In *Hamlet* the graceless usurping uncle
declares that "such divinity doth hedge a king,"
that treason cannot endanger his life.   But the
speaker is run through the body very soon after the
brag escapes his lips.

Shakespeare is no comfortable theorist, no re-
specter of orthodox doctrine, no smooth-tongued
approver of fashionable dogma.   His acute intellect

cuts away all the cobwebs, all the illusions, all the delusions, of formulæ. His untutored insight goes down to the root of things; his king is not Philosopher Bacon's "mortal god on earth"; his king is "but a man as I am," doomed to drag out a large part of his existence in the galling chains of "tradition, form and ceremonious duty," of unreality and self-deception.

Shakespeare's intuitive power of seeing things as they are, affects his attitude to all social convention. Not merely royal rulers of men are in a false position, ethically and logically. "Beware of appearances," is Shakespeare's repeated warning to men and women of all ranks in the political or social hierarchy. "Put not your trust in ornament, be it of gold or of silver." In the spheres of law and religion, the dramatist warns against pretence, against shows of virtue, honesty, or courage which have no solid backing.

> The world is still deceiv'd with ornament.
> In law what plea so tainted and corrupt
> But, being season'd with a gracious voice,
> Obscures the show of evil? In religion
> What damned error, but some sober brow
> Will bless it and approve it with a text,
> Hiding the grossness with fair ornament?
> There is no vice so simple but assumes
> Some mark of virtue on his outward parts:
> How many cowards, whose hearts are all as false
> As stairs of sand, wear yet upon their chins
> The beards of Hercules and frowning Mars,
> Who, inward searched, have livers white as milk.
> —*Merchant of Venice*, III., ii., 74–86.

Shakespeare was no cynic. He was not unduly distrustful of his fellow-men. He was not always suspecting them of something indistinguishable from fraud. When he wrote, "The world is still deceived with ornament" which "obscures the show of evil," he was expressing downright hatred—not suspicion —of sham, of quackery, of cant. His is the message of all commanding intellects which see through the hearts of men. Shakespeare's message is Carlyle's message or Ruskin's message anticipated by near- ly three centuries, and more potently and wisely phrased.

IV

At the same time as Shakespeare insists on the highest and truest standard of public duty, he, with characteristically practical insight, acknowledges no less emphatically the necessity or duty of obedience to duly regulated governments. There may appear inconsistency in first conveying the impression that governments, or their officers, are usually unworthy of trust, and then in bidding mankind obey them implicitly. But, although logical connection be- tween the two propositions be wanting, they are each convincing in their place. Both are the out- come of a robust common-sense. Order is essential to a nation's well-being. There must be discipline in civilised communities. Officers in authority must be obeyed. These are the axiomatic bases of every social contract, and no question of the personal fit- ness of officers of state impugns their stability.

Twice does Shakespeare define in the same terms what he understands by the principle of all-com- pelling order, which is inherent in government. Twice does he elaborate the argument that precise orderly division of offices, each enjoying full and un- questioned authority, is essential to the maintenance of a state's equilibrium.

The topic was first treated in the speeches of Henry V.'s councillors:—

Exeter. For government, though high and low and lower,
    Put into parts, doth keep in one consent,
    Congreeing in a full and natural close,
    Like music.
Cant.   Therefore doth heaven divide
    The state of man in divers functions,
    Setting endeavour in continual motion;
    To which is fixèd, as an aim or butt,
    Obedience: for so work the honey-bees,
    Creatures that by a rule in nature teach
    The act of order to a peopled kingdom.
                        —*Henry V.*, I., ii., 180–9.

There follows a very suggestive comparison between the commonwealth of bees and the economy of human society. The well-worn comparison has been fashioned anew by a writer of genius of our own day, M. Mæterlinck.

In *Troilus and Cressida* (I., iii., 85 *seq.*) Shakespeare returns to the discussion, and defines with greater precision "the specialty of rule." There he approaches nearer than anywhere else in his writings the sphere of strict philosophic exposition. He argues that:—

    The heavens themselves, the planets, and this centre,
    Observe degree, priority, and place,
    Insisture, course, proportion, season, form,
    Office, and custom in all line of order.

Human society is bound to follow this celestial example. At all hazards, one must protect "the unity and married calm of states." Degree, order, discipline, are the only sure safeguards against brute force and chaos which civilised institutions exist to hold in check:—

    How could communities,
    Degrees in schools and brotherhoods in cities,

Peaceful commerce from dividable shores,
The primogeniture and due of birth,
Prerogative of age, crowns, sceptres, laurels,
But by degree stand in authentic place?
Take but degree away, untune that string,
And, hark, what discord follows! each thing meets
In mere oppugnancy: the bounded waters
Should lift their bosoms higher than the shores,
And make a sop of all this solid globe:
Strength should be lord of imbecility,
And the rude son should strike his father dead:
Force should be right; or rather, right and wrong,
Between whose endless jar justice resides,
Should lose their names, and so should justice too.
Then every thing includes itself in power,
Power into will, will into appetite;
And appetite, an universal wolf,
So doubly seconded with will and power,
Must make perforce an universal prey,
And last eat up himself.

Deprived of degree, rank, order, society dissolves
itself in "chaos."

Near the end of his career, Shakespeare impres-
sively re-stated his faith in the imperative need of
the due recognition of social rank and grade in
civilised communities. In *Cymbeline* (IV., ii., 246-9)
"a queen's son" meets his death in fight with an inferior, and the conqueror is inclined to spurn the
lifeless corpse. But a wise veteran solemnly uplifts
his voice to forbid the insult. Appeal is made to the
sacred principle of social order, which must be respected even in death:—

Though mean and mighty, rotting
Together, make one dust; yet reverence,—
That angel of the world,—doth make distinction
Of place 'twixt high and low.

"Reverence, that angel of the world," is the
ultimate bond of civil society, and can never be

defied with impunity. It is the saving sanction of
social order.

V

I have quoted some of Shakespeare's avowedly
ethical utterances which bear on conditions of civil
society—on morals in their social aspect. There is
no obscurity about their drift. Apart from ethical
declaration, it may be that ethical lessons touching
political virtue as well as other specific aspects of
morality are deducible from a study of Shakespeare's
plots and characters. Very generous food for reflection seems to be offered the political philosopher by
the plots and characters of *Julius Cæsar* and *Coriolanus*. The personality of Hamlet is instinct with
ethical suggestion. The story and personages of
Measure for Measure present the most persistent of
moral problems. But discussion of the ethical im-
port of Shakespeare's several dramatic portraits or
stories is of doubtful utility. There is a genuine
danger of reading into Shakespeare's plots and
characters more direct ethical significance than is
really there. Dramatic art never consciously nor
systematically serves obvious purposes of morality,
save to its own detriment.

Nevertheless there is not likely to be much dis-
agreement with the general assertion that Shakespeare's plots and characters involuntarily develop
under his hand in conformity with the straight-
forward requirements of moral law. He upholds the
broad canons of moral truth with consistency, even
with severity. There is no mistaking in his works
on which side lies the right. He never renders vice
amiable. His want of delicacy, his challenges of
modesty, need no palliation. It was characteristic

of his age to speak more plainly of many topics about
which polite lips are nowadays silent. But Shakespeare's coarsenesses do no injury to the healthy-
minded. They do not encourage evil propensities.
Wickedness is always wickedness in Shakespeare,
and never deludes the spectator by masquerading as
something else. His plays never present problems as
to whether vice is not after all in certain conditions
the sister of virtue. Shakespeare never shows vice
in the twilight, nor leaves the spectator or reader in
doubt as to what its features precisely are. Vice
injures him who practises it in the Shakespearean
world, and ultimately proves his ruin. One cannot
play with vice with impunity.

> The gods are just, and of our pleasant vices
> Make instruments to plague us.

It is not because Shakespeare is a conscious
moralist, that the wheel comes full circle in his
dramatic world. It is because his sense of art is
involuntarily coloured by a profound conviction of
the ultimate justice which governs the operations of
human nature and society.

Shakespeare argues, in effect, that a man reaps as
he sows. It may be contended that Nature does not
always work in strict accord with this Shakespearean
canon, and that Shakespeare thereby shows himself
more of a deliberate moralist than Nature herself.
But the dramatist idealises or generalises human experience; he does not reproduce it literally. There
is nothing in the Shakespearean canon that runs
directly counter to the idealised or generalised experience of the outer world. The wicked and the
foolish, the intemperate and the over-passionate,
reach in Shakespeare's world that disastrous goal,

which nature at large keeps in reserve for them and only by rare accident suffers them to evade. The father who brings up his children badly and yet expects every dutiful consideration from them is only in rare conditions spared the rude awakening which overwhelms King Lear. The jealous husband who wrongly suspects his wife of infidelity commonly suffers the fate either of Othello or of Leontes.

VI

Shakespeare regards it as the noblest ambition in man to master his own destiny. There are numerous passages in which the dramatist figures as an absolute and uncompromising champion of the freedom of the will. "'Tis in ourselves that we are thus or thus," says one of his characters, Iago; "Our bodies are our gardens, to the which our wills are gardeners." Edmond says much the same in *King Lear* when he condemns as "the excellent foppery of the world" the ascription to external influences of all our faults and misfortunes, whereas they proceed from our wilful, deliberate choice of the worser way. Repeatedly does Shakespeare assert that we are useful or useless members of society according as we will it ourselves.

> Our remedies oft in ourselves do lie
> Which we ascribe to heaven; the fated sky
> Gives us free scope,

says Helena in *All's Well* (I., i., 231–3).

> Men at some time are masters of their fates,

says Cassius in *Julius Cæsar* (I., ii., 139–41);

> The fault, dear Brutus, is not in our stars,
> But in ourselves that we are underlings.

Hereditary predispositions, the accidents of environment, are not insuperable; they can be neutralised by force of will, by character. Character is omnipotent.

The self-sufficing, imperturbable will is the ideal possession, beside which all else in the world is valueless. But the quest of it is difficult, and success in the pursuit is rare. Mastery of the will is the result of a rare conjunction—a perfect commingling of blood and judgment. Without such harmonious union man is "a pipe"—a musical instrument—"for Fortune's finger to sound what stop she pleases." Man can only work out his own salvation when he can control his passions and can take with equal thanks Fortune's buffets or rewards.

The best of men is—

> Spare in diet
> Free from gross passion or of mirth or anger,
> Constant in spirit, not swerving with the blood.
> —*Henry V.*, II., ii., 131–3.

His is   the nature
> Whom passion could not shake—whose solid virtue
> The shot of accident nor dart of chance
> Could neither graze nor pierce.
> —*Othello*, IV., i., 176–9.

Stability of temperament is the finest fruit of the free exercise of the will; it is the noblest of masculine excellences.

> Give me that man
> That is not passion's slave, and I will wear him
> In my heart's core—ay, in my heart of hearts.
> —*Hamlet*, III., ii., 76–8.

In spite of his many beautiful portrayals of the charms and tenderness and innocence of womanhood, Shakespeare had less hope in the ultimate capacity of women to control their destiny than in the ultimate capacity of men. The greatest of his female creations, Lady Macbeth and Cleopatra, stand in a category of their own. They do not lack high power of will, even if they are unable so to commingle blood and judgment as to master fate.

Elsewhere, the dramatist seems to betray private suspicion of the normal woman's volitional capacity by applying to her heart and mind the specific epithet "waxen." The feminine mind takes the impress of its environment as easily as wax takes the impress of a seal. In two passages where this simile is employed,[1] the deduction from it is pressed to the furthest limit, and free-will is denied women altogether. Feminine susceptibility is pronounced to be incurable; wavering, impressionable emotion is a main constituent of woman's being; women are not responsible for the sins they commit nor the wrongs they endure.

This is reactionary doctrine, and one of the few points in Shakespeare's "natural" philosophy which invites dissent. But he makes generous amends by ascribing to women a plentiful supply of humour. No writer has proclaimed more effectively his faith in woman's brilliance of wit nor in her quickness of apprehension.

[1] For men have marble, *women waxen minds,*
And therefore are they formed as marble will;
The weak oppress'd, the impression of strange kinds
Is form'd in them by force, by fraud, or skill.
Then call them not the authors of their ill,
No more than wax shall be accounted evil,
Wherein is stamp'd the semblance of a devil.
—*Lucrece*, 1240–6.

How easy it is for the proper-false
In *women's waxen hearts* to set their forms!
Alas! our frailty is the cause, not we;
For, such as we are made of, such we be.
—*Twelfth Night*, II., ii., 31.

VII

Despite the solemnity which attaches to Shake-speare's philosophic reflections, he is at heart an optimist and a humorist. He combines with his serious thought a thorough joy in life, an irremovable preference for the bright over the dismal side of things. The creator of Falstaff and Mercutio, of Beatrice and the Princess in *Love's Labour's Lost*, could hardly fail to set store by that gaiety of spirit which is the antidote to unreasoning discontent, and keeps society in good savour.

> Dost thou think, because thou art virtuous,
> There shall be no more cakes and ale?

is the voice of Shakespeare as well as of Sir Toby Belch. The dramatist was at one with Rosalind, his offspring, when she told Jaques:—

> I had rather have a fool to make me merry,
> Than experience to make me sad.

The same sanguine optimistic temper constantly strikes a more impressive note.

> There is some soul of goodness in things evil,
> Would men observingly distil it out,

is a comprehensive maxim, which sounds as if it came straight from Shakespeare's lips. This battle-cry of invincible optimism is uttered in the play by Shakespeare's favourite hero, Henry V. It is hard to quarrel with the inference that these words convey the ultimate verdict of the dramatist on human affairs.

VIII

SHAKESPEARE AND PATRIOTISM [1]

His noble negligences teach
What others' toils despair to reach.

I

PATRIOTISM is a natural instinct closely allied to the domestic affections. Its normal activity is as essential as theirs to the health of society. But, in a greater degree than other instincts, the patriotic impulse works with perilous irregularity unless it be controlled by the moral sense and the intellect.

Every student of history and politics is aware how readily the patriotic instinct, if uncontrolled by morality and reason, comes into conflict with both. Freed of moral restraint it is prone to engender a peculiarly noxious brand of spurious sentiment—the patriotism of false pretence. Bombastic masquerade of the genuine impulse is not uncommon among place-hunters in Parliament and popularity-hunters in constituencies, and the honest instinct is thereby brought into disrepute. Dr Johnson was thinking solely of the frauds and moral degradation which have been sheltered by self-seekers under the name of patriotism when he none

[1] This paper was first printed in the *Cornhill Magazine*, May, 1901.

170

too pleasantly remarked: "Patriotism is the last refuge of a scoundrel."

The Doctor's epigram hardly deserves its fame. It embodies a very meagre fraction of the truth. While it ignores the beneficent effects of the patriotic instinct, it does not exhaust its evil propensities. It is not only the moral obliquity of place-hunters or popularity-hunters that can fix on patriotism the stigma of offence. Its healthy development depends on intellectual as well as on moral guidance. When the patriotic instinct, however honestly it be cherished, is freed of intellectual restraint, it works even more mischief than when it is deliberately counterfeited. Among the empty-headed it very easily degenerates into an over-assertive, a swollen selfishness, which ignores or defies the just rights and feelings of those who do not chance to be their fellow-countrymen. No one needs to be reminded how much wrongdoing and cruelty have been encouraged by perfectly honest patriots who lack "intellectual armour." Dr Johnson knew that the blockhead seeks the shelter of patriotism with almost worse result to the body politic than the scoundrel.

On the other hand, morality and reason alike resent the defect of patriotism as stoutly as its immoral or unintellectual extravagances. A total lack of the instinct implies an abnormal development of moral sentiment or intellect which must be left to the tender mercies of the mental pathologist. The man who is the friend of every country but his own can only be accounted for scientifically as the victim of an aberration of mind or heart. Ostentatious disclaimers of the patriotic sentiment deserve as little sympathy as the false pretenders to an exaggerated share of it.   A great statesman is responsible for an apophthegm on that aspect of the topic which always deserves to be quoted in the same breath as Dr Johnson's familiar half-truth.   When Sir Francis Burdett, the Radical leader in the early days of the last century, avowed scorn for the normal instinct of patriotism, Lord John Russell, the leader of the Liberal party in the House of Commons, sagely retorted: "The honourable member talks of the *cant* of patriotism; but there is something worse than the *cant* of patriotism, and that is the *recant* of patriotism." [1]   Mr Gladstone declared Lord John's repartee to be the best that he ever heard.

It may be profitable to consider how patriotism, which is singularly liable to distortion and perversion, presented itself to the mind of Shakespeare, the clearest-headed student of human thought and sentiment.

II

In Shakespeare's universal survey of human nature it was impossible that he should leave patriotism and the patriotic instinct out of account. It was inevitable that prevalent phases of both should frequently occupy his attention.   In his rôle of dramatist he naturally dealt with the topic incidentally or disconnectedly rather than in the way

[1] The pun on " cant " and " recant " was not original, though Lord John's application of it was.   Its inventor seems to have been Lady Townshend, the brilliant mother of Charles Townshend, the elder Pitt's Chancellor of the Exchequer.   When she was asked if George Whitefield, the evangelical preacher, had yet recanted, she replied: " No, he has only been canting."

of definite exposition; but in the result, his treatment will probably be found to be more exhaustive than that of any other English writer. The Shakespearean drama is peculiarly fertile in illustration of the virtuous or beneficent working of the patriotic instinct; but it does not neglect the malevolent or morbid symptoms incident either to its exorbitant or to its defective growth; nor is it wanting in suggestions as to how its healthy development may be best ensured. Part of Shakespeare's message on the subject is so well known that readers may need an apology for reference to it; but Shakespeare's declarations have not, as far as I know, been co-ordinated.[1]

Broadly speaking, the Shakespearean drama enforces the principle that an active instinct of patriotism promotes righteous conduct. This principle lies at the root of Shakespeare's treatment of history and political action, both English and Roman. Normal manifestations of the instinct in Shakespeare's world shed a gracious light on life. But it is seen to work in many ways. The patriotic instinct gives birth to various moods. It operates with some appearance of inconsistency. Now it acts as a spiritual sedative, now as a spiritual stimulant.

Of all Shakespeare's characters, it is Bolingbroke in *Richard II.* who betrays most effectively the tranquilising influence of patriotism. In him the patriotic instinct inclines to identity with the simple spirit of domesticity. It is a magnified love for

---

[1] In passing cursorily over the whole field I must ask pardon for dwelling occasionally on ground that is in detached detail sufficiently well trodden, as well as for neglecting some points which require more thorough exploration than is practicable within my present limits.

his own hearthstone — a glorified home-sickness.
The very soil of England, England's ground, excites
in Bolingbroke an overmastering sentiment of devotion.   His main happiness in life resides in the
thought that England is his mother and his nurse.
The patriotic instinct thus exerts on a character
which is naturally cold and unsympathetic a soften-
ing, soothing, and purifying sway.   Despite his for-
bidding self-absorption and personal ambition he
touches hearts, and rarely fails to draw tears when
he sighs forth the bald lines:—

> Where'er I wander, boast of this I can,
> Though banished, yet a true-born Englishman.

In such a shape the patriotic instinct may tend in
natures weaker than Bolingbroke's to mawkishness
or sentimentality.   But it is incapable of active
offence.   It makes for the peace and goodwill not
merely of nations among themselves, but of the constituent elements of each nation within itself.   It
unifies human aspiration and breeds social harmony.

Very different is the phase of the patriotic instinct
which is portrayed in the more joyous, more frank,
and more impulsive characters of Faulconbridge
the Bastard in the play of *King John,* and of the
King in *Henry V.*   It is in them an inexhaustible
stimulus to action.   It is never quiescent, but its
operations are regulated by morality and reason,
and it finally induces a serene exaltation of temper.
It was a pardonable foible of Elizabethan writers
distinctly to identify with the English character
this healthy energetic sort of patriotism—the sort of
patriotism to which an atmosphere of knavery or
folly proves fatal.

Faulconbridge is an admirable embodiment of the patriotic sentiment in its most attractive guise. He is a manly soldier, blunt in speech, contemning subterfuge, chafing against the dictates of political expediency, and believing that quarrels between nations which cannot be accommodated without loss of self-respect on the one side or the other, had better be fought out in resolute and honourable war. He is the sworn foe of the bully or the braggart. Cruelty is hateful to him. The patriotic instinct nurtures in him a warm and generous humanity. His faith in the future of his nation depends on the confident hope that she will be true to herself, to her traditions, to her responsibilities, to the great virtues; that she will be at once courageous and magnanimous:—

> Come the three corners of the world in arms,
> And we shall shock them. Nought shall make us rue,
> If England to itself do rest but true.

Faulconbridge's patriotism is a vivacious spur to good endeavour in every relation of life.

Henry V. is drawn by Shakespeare at fuller length than Faulconbridge. His character is cast in a larger mould. But his patriotism is of the same spirited, wholesome type. Though Henry is a born soldier, he discourages insolent aggression or reckless displays of prowess in fight. With greater emphasis than his archbishops and bishops he insists that his country's sword should not be unsheathed except at the bidding of right and conscience. At the same time, he is terrible in resolution when the time comes for striking blows. War, when it is once invoked, must be pursued with all possible force and fury:—

> In peace there's nothing so becomes a man
> As modest stillness and humility.
> But when the blast of war blows in his ears,
> Then imitate the action of the tiger.[1]

But although Henry's patriotic instinct can drive him into battle, it keeps him faithful there to the paths of humanity. Always alive to the horrors of war, he sternly forbids looting or even the use of insulting language to the enemy. It is only when a defeated enemy declines to acknowledge the obvious ruin of his fortunes that a sane and practical patriotism defends resort on the part of the conqueror to the grimmest measure of severity. The healthy instinct stiffens the grip on the justly won fruits of victory. As soon as Henry V. sees that the French wilfully deny the plain fact of their overthrow, he is moved, quite consistently, to exclaim:—

> What is it then to me if impious war,
> Arrayed in flames like to the prince of fiends,
> Do with his smirched complexion all fell feats,
> Enlinked to waste and desolation?

The context makes it clear that there is no confusion here between the patriotic instinct and mere bellicose ecstasy.

The confusion of patriotism with militant aggressiveness is as familiar to the Shakespearean drama as to the external world; but it is always exhibited by Shakespeare in its proper colours. The Shakespearean "mob," unwashed in mind and body,

---

[1] On this point the Shakespearean oracle always speaks with a decisive and practical note:—

> Beware
> Of entrance to a quarrel, but being in
> Bear't that the opposed may beware of thee.
> —*Hamlet*, I., iii., 65–7.

habitually yields to it, and justifies itself by a spe-
ciousness of argument against which a clean vision
rebels. The so-called patriotism which seeks expression in war for its own sake is alone intelligible
to Shakespeare's pavement orators. "Let me have
war, say I," exclaims the professedly patriotic
spokesman of the ill-conditioned proletariat in *Coriolanus;* "it exceeds peace as far as day does night; it's
spritely, waking, audible, and full of vent. Peace is a
very apoplexy, lethargy; mulled, deaf, sleepy, insen-
sible. . . . Ay, and it makes men hate one another."
For this distressing result of peace, the reason is given
that in times of peace men have less need of one
another than in seasons of war, and the crude argument closes with the cry: "The wars for my money."
There is irony in this suggestion of the mercantile
value of war on the lips of a spokesman of paupers.
It is solely the impulsive mindless patriot who strains
after mere military glory.

> Glory is like a circle in the water,
> Which never ceaseth to enlarge itself,
> Till by broad spreading it disperse to nought.
> —1 *Henry VI.,* I., ii., 133–5.

No wise man vaunts in the name of patriotism
his own nation's superiority over another. The
typical patriot, Henry V., once makes the common
boast that one Englishman is equal to three Frenchmen, but he apologises for the brag as soon as it is
out of his mouth. (He fears the air of France has
demoralised him.)

Elsewhere Shakespeare utters a vivacious warning against the patriot's exclusive claim for his
country of natural advantages, which all the world
shares substantially alike.

> Hath Britain all the sun that shines? Day, night,
> Are they not but in Britain? I' the world's volume
> Our Britain seems as of it, but not in 't;
> In a great pool, a swan's nest: pr'ythee, think
> There's livers out of Britain.[1]

It is not the wild hunger for war, but the stable interests of peace that are finally subserved in the Shakespearean world by true and well-regulated patriotism. *Henry V.*, the play of Shakespeare which shows the genuine patriotic instinct in its most energetic guise, ends with a powerful appeal to France and England, traditional foes, to cherish "neighbourhood and Christianlike accord," so that never again should "war advance his bleeding sword 'twixt England and fair France."

However whole-heartedly Shakespeare rebukes the excesses and illogical pretensions to which the lack of moral or intellectual discipline exposes patriotism, he reserves his austerest censure for the disavowal of the patriotic instinct altogether. One of the greatest of his plays is practically a diagnosis of the perils which follow in the train of a wilful abnegation of the normal instinct. In *Coriolanus* Shakespeare depicts the career of a man who thinks that he can, by virtue of inordinate self-confidence and belief in his personal superiority over the rest of his countrymen, safely abjure and defy the common patriotic instinct, which, after all, keeps the State in being. "I'll never," says Coriolanus,

> Be such a gosling to obey instinct, but stand
> As if a man were author of himself,
> And knew no other kin.[2]

Coriolanus deliberately suppresses the patriotic instinct, and, with greater consistency than others who

---

[1] *Cymbeline*, III., iv., 139–43.   [2] *Coriolanus*, V., iii., 34–7.

have at times followed his example, joins the fighting ranks of his country's enemies by way of illus-
trating his sincerity. His action proves to be in
conflict with the elementary condition of social
equilibrium. The subversion of the natural instinct
is brought to the logical issues of sin and death.
Domestic ties are rudely severed. The crime of
treason is risked with an insolence that is fatal
to the transgressor. With relentless logic does the
Shakespearean drama condemn defiance of the natural instinct of patriotism.

III

It does not, however, follow that the patriotic
instinct of the Shakespearean gospel encourages
blind adoration of state or country. Intelligent citizens of the Shakespearean world are never prohibited
from honestly criticising the acts or aspirations of
their fellows, and from seeking to change them when
they honestly think they can be changed for the
better. It is not the business of a discerning patriot
to sing pæans in his nation's honour. His final aim
is to help his country to realise the highest ideals of
social and political conduct which are known to him,
and to ensure for her the best possible "reputation
through the world." Criticism conceived in a patriotic spirit should be constant and unflagging.
The true patriot speaks out as boldly when he thinks
the nation errs as when, in his opinion, she adds new
laurels to her crown. The Shakespearean patriot
applies a rigorous judgment to all conditions of his
environment—both social and political.

Throughout the English history plays, Shakespeare bears convincing testimony to the right, and

even to the duty, of the patriot to exercise in all
seriousness his best powers of criticism on the political
conduct of his fellow-citizens and of those who rule
over him.

Shakespeare's studies of English history are ani-
mated by a patriotism which boldly seeks and faces
the truth. His dramatic presentments of English
history have been often described as fragments of a
national epic, as detached books of an English *Iliad*.
But they embody no epic or heroic glorification of
the nation. Taking the great series which begins
chronologically with *King John* and ends with
Richard III. (*Henry VIII*. stands apart), we find
that Shakespeare makes the central features of the
national history the persons of the kings. Only in
the case of *Henry V*. does he clothe an English king
with any genuine heroism. Shakespeare's kings are
as a rule but men as we are. The violet smells to
them as it does to us; all their senses have but
human conditions; and though their affections be
higher mounted than ours, yet when they stoop they
stoop with like wing. Excepting *Henry V*., the history plays are tragedies. They "tell sad stories of
the death of kings." But they do not merely illustrate the crushing burdens of kingship or point the
moral of the hollowness of kingly pageantry; they
explain why kingly glory is in its essence brittle
rather than brilliant. And since Shakespeare's rulers
reflect rather than inspire the character of the nation,
we are brought to a study of the causes of the
brittleness of national glory.

The glory of a nation, as of a king, is only stable,
we learn, when the nation, as the king, lives soberly,
virtuously and wisely, and is courageous, magnan-

imous, and zealous after knowledge. Cowardice, meanness, ignorance, and cruelty ruin nations as surely as they ruin kings. This is the lesson specifically taught in the most eloquent of all the direct avowals of patriotism which are to be found in Shakespeare's plays—in the dying speech of John of Gaunt.

That speech is no ebullition of the undisciplined patriotic instinct. It is a solemn announcement of the truth that the greatness and glory, with which nature and history have endowed a nation, may be dissipated when, on the one hand, the rulers prove selfish, frivolous and unequal to the responsibilities which a great past places on their shoulders, and when, on the other hand, the nation acquiesces in the depravity of its governors. In his opening lines, the speaker lays emphasis on the possibilities of greatness with which the natural physical conditions of the country and its political and military traditions have invested his countrymen. Thereby he brings into lurid relief the sin and the shame of paltering with, of putting to ignoble uses, the national character and influence. The dying patriot apostrophises England in the familiar phrases, as:—

> This royal throne of kings, this sceptred isle. . . .
> This fortress, built by nature for herself,
> Against infection and the hand of war;
> This happy breed of men, this little world;
> This precious stone set in the silver sea,
> Which serves it in the office of a wall,
> Or as a moat defensive to a house,
> Against the envy of less happier lands:
> This blessed plot, this earth, this realm, this England,
> This land of such dear souls, this dear, dear land,
> Dear for her reputation through the world.
> —*Richard II.*, II., i., 40–58.

The last line identifies with the patriotic instinct the

aspiration of a people to deserve well of foreign
opinion. Subsequently the speaker turns from his
survey of the ideal which he would have his country
seek. He exposes with ruthless frankness the ugly
realities of her present degradation.

> England, bound in with the triumphant sea,
> Whose rocky shore beats back the envious siege
> Of wat'ry Neptune, is now bound in with shame,
> With inky blots, and rotten parchment bonds,—
> That England, that was wont to conquer others,
> Hath made a shameful conquest of itself.
>   —*Richard II.*, II., i., 61–6.

At the moment the speaker's warning is scorned, but
ultimately it takes effect. At the end of the play of
Richard II., England casts off the ruler and his allies,
who by their self-indulgence and moral weakness
play false with the traditions of the country.

In *Henry V.*, the only one of Shakespeare's historical plays in which an English king quits the stage
in the full enjoyment of prosperity, his good fortune
is more than once explained as the reward of his
endeavour to abide by the highest ideals of his race,
and of his resolve to exhibit in his own conduct its
noblest mettle. His strongest appeals to his fellow-
countrymen are:—

> Dishonour not your mothers; now attest
> That those whom you call'd fathers did beget you;
>
> .   .   .   .   .
>
>   Let us swear
> That you are worth your breeding.

The kernel of sound patriotism is respect for a
nation's traditional repute, for the attested worth of
the race. That is the large lesson which Shakespeare taught continuously throughout his career as
a dramatist. The teaching is not solely enshrined
in the poetic eloquence either of plays of his early

years like *Richard II.*, or of plays of his middle life
like *Henry V.* It is the last as well as the first word
in Shakespeare's collective declaration on the true
character of patriotism. *Cymbeline* belongs to the
close of his working life, and there we meet once
more the assurance that a due regard to the past
and an active resolve to keep alive ancestral virtue
are the surest signs of health in the patriotic instinct.

The accents of John of Gaunt were repeated by
Shakespeare with little modulation at that time of
his life when his reflective power was at its ripest.
The Queen of Britain, Cymbeline's wife, is the personage in whose mouth Shakespeare sets, not perhaps quite appropriately, the latest message in regard
to patriotism that he is known to have delivered.
Emissaries from the Emperor Augustus have come
from Rome to demand from the King of Britain payment of the tribute that Julius Cæsar had long since
imposed on the island, by virtue of a *force majeure*,
which is temporarily extinguished. The pusillani-
mous King Cymbeline is indisposed to put himself to
the pains of contesting the claim, but the resolute
queen awakens in him a sense of patriotism and of
patriotic obligation by recalling the more nobly inspired attitude of his ancestors, and by convincing
him of the baseness of ignoring the physical features
which had been bestowed by nature on his domains
as a guarantee of their independence.

> Remember, sir my liege,
> The kings your ancestors, together with
> The natural bravery of your isle, which stands
> As Neptune's park, ribbed and paled in
> With rocks unscalable and roaring waters,
> With sands, that will not bear your enemies' boats,
> But suck them up to the topmast.
>
> —*Cymbeline*, III., i., 16–22.

The appeal prevails, and the tribute is refused.
Although the evolution of the plot which is based on
an historical chronicle compels the renewed acqui-
escence of the British king in the Roman tax at the
close of the play, the Queen of Britain's spirited
insistence on the maritime strength of her country
loses little of its significance.

IV

Frank criticism of the social life of the nation
is as characteristic of Shakespearean drama as out-
spoken exposition of its political failings. There is
hardly any of Shakespeare's plays which does not
offer shrewd comment on the foibles and errors of
contemporary English society.

To society Shakespeare's attitude is that of a
humourist, who invites to reformation half-jestingly.
His bantering tone, when he turns to social censure,
strikingly contrasts with the tragic earnestness that
colours his criticism of political vice or weakness.
Some of the national failings on the social side which
Shakespeare rebukes may seem trivial at a first
glance. But it is the voice of prudent patriotism
which prompts each count in the indictment. The
keenness of Shakespeare's insight is attested by the
circumstance that every charge has a modern application. None is yet quite out of date.

Shakespeare rarely missed an opportunity of
betraying contempt for the extravagances of his
countrymen and countrywomen in regard to dress.
Portia says of her English suitor Faulconbridge, the
young baron of England: "How oddly he is suited!
I think he bought his doublet in Italy, his round hose

in France, his bonnet in Germany, and his behaviour everywhere." Another failing in Englishmen, which Portia detects in her English suitor, is a total ignorance of any language but his own. She, an Italian lady, remarks: "You know I say nothing to him, for he understands not me nor I him. He hath neither Latin, French, nor Italian. He is a proper man's picture, but, alas! who can converse with a dumb show." This moving plaint draws attention to a defect which is not yet supplied. There are few Englishmen nowadays who, on being challenged to court Portia in Italian, would not cut a sorry figure in dumb show—sorrier figures than Frenchmen or Germans. No true patriot ought to ignore the fact or to direct attention to it with complacency.

Again, Shakespeare was never unmindful of the intemperate habits of his compatriots. When Iago sings a verse of the song beginning, "And let me the cannikin clink," and ending, "Why then let a soldier drink," Cassio commends the excellence of the ditty. Thereupon Iago explains: "I learned it in England, where indeed, they are most potent in potting: Your Dane, your German, and your swag-bellied Hollander —Drink, ho!—are nothing to your English." Cassio asks: "Is your Englishman so expert in his drinking?" Iago retorts: "Why, he drinks you, with facility, your Dane dead drunk," and gains, the speaker explains, easy mastery over the German and the Hollander.

A further stroke of Shakespeare's social criticism hits the thoughtless pursuit of novelty, which infected the nation and found vent in Shakespeare's day in the patronage of undignified shows and sports. When Trinculo, perplexed by the outward aspect of

the hideous Caliban, mistakes him for a fish, he remarks: "Were I in England now, as once I was, and
had but this fish painted, not a holiday fool there
but would give a piece of silver: there would this
monster make a man; any strange beast there makes
a man: when they will not give a doit to relieve a
lame beggar, they will lay out ten to see a dead
Indian."

Shakespeare seems s., y to confess a personal
conviction of defective balance in the popular judgment when he makes the first grave-digger remark
that Hamlet was sent into England because he was
mad.

"He shall recover his wits there," the old clown
suggests, "or if he do not, 'tis no great matter there."

"Why?" asks Hamlet.

"'Twill not be seen in him there; there the men
are as mad as he."

So, too, in the emphatically patriotic play of
Henry V., Shakespeare implies that he sees some
purpose in the Frenchman's jibes at the foggy, raw,
and dull climate of England, which engenders in its
inhabitants, the Frenchman argues, a frosty temperament, an ungenial coldness of blood.   Nor does the
dramatist imply dissent from the French marshal's
suggestion that Englishmen's great meals of beef
impair the efficiency of their intellectual armour.
The point of the reproof is not blunted by the subsequent admission of a French critic in the same
scene to the effect that, however robustious and
rough in manner Englishmen may be, they have
the unmatchable courage of the English breed of
mastiffs.   To credit men with the highest virtues of
which dogs are capable is a grudging compliment.

V

To sum up. The Shakespearean drama enjoins
those who love their country wisely to neglect no
advantage that nature offers in the way of resisting
unjust demands upon it; to remember that her
prosperity depends on her command of the sea,—
of "the silver sea, which serves it in the office of a
wall, or as a moat defensive to a house against the
envy of less happier lands"; to hold firm in the
memory "the dear souls" who have made "her
reputation through the world"; to subject at need
her faults and frailties to criticism and rebuke; and
finally to treat with disdain those in places of power,
who make of no account their responsibilities to the
past as well as to the present and the future. The
political, social, and physical conditions of his
country have altered since Shakespeare lived. England has ceased to be an island-power. The people
rule instead of the king. Social responsibilities
are more widely acknowledged. But the dramatist's doctrine of patriotism has lost little of its
pristine vitality, and is relevant to current affairs.

IX

A PERIL OF SHAKESPEAREAN
RESEARCH [1]

FOR some years past scarcely a month passes without
my receipt of a communication from a confiding
stranger, to the effect that he has discovered some
piece of information concerning Shakespeare which
has hitherto eluded research.   Very often has a correspondent put himself to the trouble of forwarding
a photograph of the title-page of a late sixteenth or
early seventeenth century book, on which has been
scrawled in old-fashioned script the familiar name of
William Shakespeare.   At intervals, which seem to
recur with mathematical regularity, I receive intelligence that a portrait of the poet, of which nothing is
hitherto known, has come to light in some recondite
corner of England or America, and it is usually added
that a contemporary inscription settles all doubt of
authenticity.

I wish to speak with respect and gratitude of
these confidences.   I welcome them, and have no
wish to repress them.   But truth does not permit
me to affirm that such as have yet reached me have
done more than enlarge my conception of the scope

[1] This paper was first printed in *The Author,* October, 1903.
188

of human credulity.   I look forward to the day when the postman shall, through the generosity of some appreciative reader of my biography of Shakespeare, deliver at my door an autograph of the dramatist of which nothing has been heard before, or a genuine portrait of contemporary date, the existence of which has never been suspected.   But up to the moment of writing, despite the good intentions of my correspondents, no experience of the kind has befallen me.

There is something pathetic in the frequency with which correspondents, obviously of unblemished character and most generous instinct, send me almost tearful expressions of regret that I should have hitherto ignored one particular document, which throws (in their eyes) a curious gleam on the dramatist's private life.   At least six times a year am I reminded how it is recorded in more than one obscure eighteenth-century periodical that the dramatist, George Peele, wrote to his friend Marle or Marlowe, in an extant letter, of a merry meeting which was held at a place called the "Globe." Whether the rendezvous were tavern or playhouse is left undetermined.   The assembled company, I am assured, included not merely Edward Alleyn the actor, and Ben Jonson, but Shakespeare himself. Together these celebrated men are said to have discussed a passage in the new play of *Hamlet*.   The reported talk is at the best tame prattle.   Yet, if Shakespeare be anywhere revealed in unconstrained intercourse with professional associates, no biographer deserves pardon for overlooking the revelation, however disappointing be its purport.

Unfortunately for this neglected intelligence, the

letter in question is an eighteenth-century fabrication. It is a forgery of no intrinsic brilliance or wit. It bears on its dull face marks of guilt which could only escape the notice of the uninformed. It is not likely to mislead the critical. Nevertheless it has deceived many an uncritical reader, and has constantly found its way into print without meeting serious confutation. It may therefore be worth while setting its true origin and subsequent history on record. No endeavour is likely in all the circumstances of the case to prevent an occasional resurrection of the meagre spectre; but at present it appears to walk in various quarters quite unimpeded, and an endeavour to lay it may not be without its uses.

II

Through the first half of 1763 there was published in London a monthly magazine called the *Theatrical Review, or Annals of the Drama,* an anonymous miscellany of dramatic biography and criticism. It was a colourless contribution to the journalism of the day, and lacked powers of endurance. It ceased at the end of six months. The six instalments were re-issued as "Volume I." at the end of June 1763; but that volume had no successor.[1]

All that is worth noting of the *Theatrical Review* of 1763 now is that among its contributors was an extremely interesting personality. He was a young

---

[1] Other independent publications of similar character appeared under the identical title of *The Theatrical Review* both in 1758 and 1772. The latter collected the ephemeral dramatic criticisms of John Potter, a well-known writer for the stage.

man of good education and independent means, who
had chambers in the Temple, and was enthusiastically
applying himself to a study of Shakespeare and
Elizabethan dramatic literature. His name, George
Steevens, acquired in later years world-wide fame
as that of the most learned of Shakespearean com-
mentators. Of the real value of Steevens's scholarship no question is admissible, and his reputation
justly grew with his years. Yet Steevens's temper
was singularly perverse and mischievous. His confidence in his own powers led him to contemn the
powers of other people. He enjoyed nothing so
much as mystifying those who were engaged in the
same pursuits as himself, and his favourite method
of mystification was to announce anonymously the
discovery of documents which owed all their existence
to his own ingenuity. This, he admitted, was his
notion of "fun." Whenever the whim seized him,
he would in gravest manner reveal to the Press, or
even contrive to bring to the notice of a learned
society, some alleged relic in manuscript or in stone
which he had deliberately manufactured. His sole
aim was to recreate himself with laughter at the
perplexity that such unholy pranks aroused. It is
one of these Puck-like tricks on Steevens's part that
has spread confusion among those of my correspondents, who allege that Peele has handed down to
us a personal reminiscence of the great dramatist.

The *Theatrical Review*, in its second number,
offered an anonymous biography of the great actor
and theatrical manager of Shakespeare's day, Edward Alleyn. This biography was clearly one of
Steevens's earliest efforts. It is for the most part an
innocent compilation. But it contains one passage

in its author's characteristic vein of mischief.   Mid-
way in the essay the reader is solemnly assured that
a brand-new contemporary reference to Alleyn's
eminent associate Shakespeare was at his disposal.
The new story "carries with it" (asserts the writer)
"all the air of probability and truth, and has never
been in print before."   "A gentleman of honour and
veracity," run the next sentences, which were designed to put the unwary student off his guard, "in
the commission of the peace for Middlesex, has shown
us a letter dated in the year 1600, which he assures
us has been in the possession of his family, by the
mother's side, for a long series of years, and which
bears all the marks of antiquity."   The superscrip-
tion was interpreted to run: "For Master Henrie
Marle, livynge at the sygne of the rose by the palace."

There follows at length the paper of which the
family of the honourable and veracious gentleman
"in the commission of the peace for Middlesex"
had become possessed "by the mother's side."   The
words were these:—

"FRIENDE MARLE,
          "I must desyre that my syster hyr
watche, and the cookerie booke you promysed, may
be sent by the man.   I never longed for thy company
more than last night; we were all very merrye at the
Globe, when Ned Alleyn did not scruple to affyrme
pleasantely to thy friend Will, that he had stolen his
speech about the qualityes of an actor's excellencye,
in *Hamlet* hys tragedye, from conversations many-
fold which had passed between them, and opinyons
given by Allen touchinge the subject.   Shakespeare
did not take this talke in good sorte; but Jonson put
an end to the stryfe with wittielie saying: "This
affaire needeth no contentione; you stole it from

Ned, no doubt; do not marvel; have you not seen
him act tymes out of number"?

    "Believe me most syncerelie,
            "Harrie,
                "Thyne,
                    "G. PEEL."

The text of this strangely-spelt, strangely-worded
epistle, with its puny efforts at a jest, was succeeded
by a suggestion that "G. Peel," the alleged signatory,
could be none other than George Peele, the dramatist, who achieved reputation in Shakespeare's early
days, and was an industrious collector of anecdotes.

Thus the impish Steevens baited his hook. The
sport which followed must have exceeded his ex-
pectations. Any one familiar with the bare outline
of Elizabethan literary history should have perceived
that a trap had been set. The letter was assigned
to the year 1600. Shakespeare's play of *Hamlet*, to
the performance of which it unconcernedly refers,
was not produced before 1602; at that date George
Peele had lain full four years in his grave. Peele
could never have passed the portals of the theatre
called the "Globe"; for it was not built until 1599.
No historic tavern of the name is known. The sur-
name of the person, to whom the letter was pretend-
ed to have been addressed, is suspicious. "Marle"
was one way of spelling "Marlowe" at a period when
forms of surnames varied with the caprice of the
writer. The great dramatist, *Christopher* Marle, or
Marloe, or Marlowe, had died in 1593. "Henrie
Marle" is counterfeit coinage of no doubtful stamp.

The language and the style of the letter are undeserving of serious examination. They are of a far
later period than the Elizabethan age. They cannot

be dated earlier than 1763.   Safely might the heaviest odds be laid that in no year of the reign of Queen Elizabeth "did friende Marle promyse G. Peel his syster that he would send hyr watche and the cookerie book by the man," or that "Ned Alleyn made pleasante affirmation to G. Peel of friend Will's theft of the speech in *Hamlet* concerning an actor's excellencye."

From top to toe the imposture is obvious.   But the general reader of the eighteenth century was confiding, unsuspicious, greedy of novel information. The description of the source of the document seemed to him precise enough to silence doubt.

III

The *Theatrical Review* of 1673 succeeded in launching the fraud on a quite triumphal progress. Again and again, as the century advanced, was G. Peel's declaration to "friende Marle" paraded, without hint of its falsity, before snappers-up of Shakespearean trifles.   Seven years after its first publication, the epistle found admission in a slightly altered setting to so reputable a periodical as the *Annual Register*.   Burke was still directing that useful publication, and whatever information the *Register* shielded, was reckoned to be of veracity.   "G. Peel" and "friende Marle" were there in the year 1770, suffered to exchange their confidences in the most honourable environment.

Another seven years passed, and in 1777 there appeared an ambitious work of reference, entitled *Biographia Literaria, or a Biographical History of*

Literature, which gave its author, John Berkenhout,
a free-thinking physician, his chief claim to re-
membrance.   Steevens was a friend of Berkenhout,
and helped him in the preparation of the book.   Into
his account of Shakespeare, the credulous physician
introduced quite honestly the fourteen-year old
forgery.   The reputed date of 1600, which the sup-
posititious justice of the peace had given it in the
Theatrical Review, was now suppressed.   Berkenhout
confined his comment to the halting reminiscence:
"Whence I copied this letter I do not recollect; but
I remember that at the time of transcribing it, I had
no doubt of its authenticity."

Thrice had the trick been worked effectively in
conspicuous places before Steevens died in 1800.
But the evil that he did lived after him, and within
a year of his death the imposture renewed its youth.
A correspondent, who concealed his identity under
the signature of "Grenovicus" (*i.e.*, of Greenwich),
sent Peel's letter in 1801 to the *Gentleman's Magazine*, a massive repertory of useful knowledge.   There
it was duly reprinted in the number for June.   "Grenovicus" had the assurance to claim the letter as his
own discovery.   "To my knowledge," he wrote, "it
has never yet appeared in print."   He refrained
from indicating how he had gained access to it, but
congratulated himself and the readers of the *Gentleman's Magazine* on the valiant feast that he provided for them.   His action was apparently taken
by the readers of the *Gentleman's Magazine* at his
own valuation.

Meanwhile the discerning critic was not altogether passive.   Isaac D'Israeli denounced the fraud
in his *Curiosities of Literature;* but he and others did

their protesting gently. The fraud looked to the expert° too shamefaced to merit a vigorous onslaught. He imagined the spurious epistle must die of its own inanity. In this he miscalculated the credulity of the general reader. "Grenovicus" of the *Gentleman's Magazine* had numerous disciples.

Many a time during the past century has his exploit been repeated. Even so acute a scholar as Alexander Dyce thought it worth while to reprint the letter in 1829 in the first edition of his collected works of George Peele (Vol. I., page 111), although he declined to pledge himself to its authenticity. The latest historian of Dulwich College [1] has admitted it to his text with too mildly worded a caveat. Often more recently has "G. Peel" emerged from seclusion to darken the page of a modern popular magazine. I have met him unabashed during the present century in two literary periodicals of repute—in the *Academy* (of London), in the issue of the 18th of January, 1902, and in the *Poet Lore* (of Philadelphia), in the following April number. Future disinterments may safely be prophesied. In the jungle of the *Annual Register* or the *Gentleman's Magazine* the forgery lurks unchallenged, and there will always be inexperienced explorers, who from time to time will run the unhallowed thing to earth there, and bring it forth as a new and unsuspected truth.

Perhaps forgery is too big a word to apply to Steevens's concoction. Others worked at later periods on lines of mystification similar to his; but, unlike his disciples, he did not seek from his misdirected ingenuity pecuniary gain or even notoriety. He never set his name to this invention of "Peel" and

[1] William Young's *History of Dulwich College,* 1889, II., 41-2.

"Marle," and their insipid chatter about *Hamlet* at the "Globe." ·Steevens's sole aim was to delude the unwary. It is difficult to detect humour in the endeavour. But the perversity of the human intellect has no limits. This ungainly example of it is only worth attention because it has sailed under its false colours without very serious molestation for one hundred and forty-three years.

X

SHAKESPEARE IN FRANCE [1]

I

NOTHING but good can come of a comparative study of English and French literature. The political intercourse of the two countries has involved them in an endless series of broils. But between the literatures of the two countries friendly relations have subsisted for over five centuries. In the literary sphere the interchange of neighbourly civilities has known no interruption. The same literary forms have not appealed to the tastes of the two nations; but differences of æsthetic temperament have not prevented the literature of the one from levying substantial loans on the literature of the other, and that with a freedom and a frequency which were calculated to breed discontent between any but the most cordial of allies. While the literary geniuses of the two nations have pursued independent ideals, they have viewed as welcome courtesies the willingness and readiness of the one to borrow sustenance of the other on the road. It is unlikely that any full or formal balance-sheet of such lendings and borrowings

[1] This paper was first printed in *The Nineteenth Century*, June, 1899.

will ever be forthcoming, for it is felt instinctively
by literary accountants and their clients on both
shores of the English Channel that the debts on
the one side keep a steady pace with the debts on
the other, and there is no balance to be collected.

No recondite research is needed to establish
this general view of the situation. It is well known
how the poetic career of Chaucer, the earliest of
great English poets, was begun under French masters.
The greatest poem of mediæval France, the *Roman
de la Rose*, was turned into English by his youthful
pen, and the chief French poet of the day, Eustace
Deschamps, held out to him the hand of fellowship
in the enthusiastic *balade*, in which he apostrophised
" le grand translateur, noble Geoffroi Chaucer."
Following Chaucer's example, the great poets of
Elizabeth's reign and of James the First's reign most
liberally and most literally assimilated the verse of
their French contemporaries, Ronsard, Du Bellay,
and Desportes.[1]   Early in the seventeenth century,
Frenchmen returned the compliment by naturalising
in French translations the prose romances of Sir
Philip Sidney and Robert Greene, the philosophical
essays of Bacon, and the ethical and theological
writings of Bishop Joseph Hall. From the acces-
sion of Charles the Second until that of George
the Third, the English drama framed itself on
French models, and Pope, who long filled the throne

[1] In the Introduction to a collection of Elizabethan Sonnets,
published in Messrs Constable's re-issue of Arber's *English
Garner* (1904), the present writer has shown that numerous sonnets, which Elizabethan writers issued as original poems, were
literal translations from the French of Ronsard, Du Bellay, and
Desportes. Numerous loans of like character were levied silently
on many Italian authors.

of a literary dictator in England, acknowledged discipleship to Boileau. A little later the literary philosophers of France—Rousseau and the Encyclopédistes—drew nutrition from the writings of Hobbes and Locke. French novel-readers of the eighteenth century found their chief joy in the tearful emotions excited by the sentimentalities of Richardson and Sterne. French novel-writers one hundred and thirty years ago had small chance of recognition if they disdained to traffic in the lachrymose wares which the English novelists had brought into fashion.

At the present moment the cultured Englishman finds his most palatable fiction in the publications of Paris. Within recent memory the English playgoer viewed with impatience any theatrical programme which lacked a Parisian flavour. The late Sir Henry Irving, who, during the past generation, sought to sustain the best traditions of the English drama, produced in his last years two original plays, *Robespierre* and *Dante*, by the *doyen* of living French dramatists, M. Sardou. Complementary tendencies are visible across the Channel. The French stage often offers as cordial a reception to plays of English manufacture as is offered in London to the plays derived from France. No histrionic event attracts higher interest in Paris than the assumption by a great actor or actress of a Shakespearean rôle for the first time; and French dramatic critics have been known to generate such heat in debates over the right conception of a Shakespearean character that their differences have required adjustment at the sword's point.

Of greater interest is it to note that in all the cultivated centres of France a new and unparalleled

energy is devoted to-day to the study of English
literature of both the present and the past. The
research recently expended on the topic by French
scholars has not been excelled in Germany, and has
rarely been equalled in England. Critical biograph-
ies of James Thomson (of *The Seasons*), of Burns, of
Young, and of Wordsworth have come of late from
the pens of French professors of English literature,
and their volumes breathe a minute accuracy and
a fulness of sympathetic knowledge which are certainly not habitual to English professors of English literature. This scholarly movement in France
shows signs of rapid extension. Each summer vaca-
tion sees an increase in the number of French visitors
to the British Museum reading-room, who are engaged on recondite researches into English literary
history. The new zeal of Frenchmen for English
studies claims the most cordial acknowledgment of
English scholars, and it is appropriate that the
most coveted lectureship on English literature in an
English University—the Clark lectureship at Trinity
College, Cambridge — should have been bestowed
last year on the learned professor of English at the
Sorbonne, M. Beljame, author of *Le Public et les
Hommes de Lettres en Angleterre au XVIII*^e *Siècle.*
M. Beljame's unexpected death (on September 17,
1906), shortly after his work at Cambridge was com-
pleted, is a loss alike to English and French letters.

II

In view of the growth of the French interest in
English literary history, it was to be expected that
serious efforts should be made in France to determine the character and dimensions of the influence

exerted on French literature by the greatest of all English men of letters—by Shakespeare. That work has been undertaken by M. Jusserand. In 1898 he gave to the world the results of his investigation in his native language. Subsequently, with a welcome consideration for the linguistic incapacities of Shakespeare's countrymen, he repeated his conclusions in their tongue.[1] The English translation is embellished with many pictorial illustrations of historic interest and value.

Among French writers on English literature, M. Jusserand is the most voluminous and the most widely informed. His career differs in an important particular from that of his countrymen who pursue the same field of study. He is not by profession a teacher or writer: he is a diplomatist, and now holds the high office of French ambassador to the United States of America. M. Jusserand has treated in his books of almost all periods of English literary history, and he has been long engaged on an exhaustive *Literary History of the English People,* of which the two volumes already published bring the narrative as far as the close of the Civil Wars.

M. Jusserand enjoys the rare, although among modern Frenchmen by no means unexampled, faculty of writing with almost equal ease and felicity in both French and English. His walk in life gives him a singularly catholic outlook. His learning is profound, but he is not overburdened by it, and he preserves his native gaiety of style even when solving crabbed problems of bibliography. He is at times discursive, but he is never tedious; and he shows

[1] *Shakespeare in France under the Ancien Régime,* by J. J. Jusserand. London: T. Fisher Unwin. 1899.

no trace of that philological pedantry and narrow-
ness or obliquity of critical vision which the detailed
study of literary history has been known to breed
in English and German investigators. While M.
Jusserand betrays all the critical independence of
his compatriot, M. Taine, his habit of careful and
laborious research illustrates with peculiar vividness the progress which English scholarship has made
in France since M. Taine completed his sparkling
survey of English literature in 1864.

M. Jusserand handles the theme of *Shakespeare
in France under the Ancien Régime* with all the
lightness of touch and wealth of minute detail to
which he has accustomed his readers. Nowhere
have so many facts been brought together in order
to illustrate the literary intercourse of Frenchmen
and Englishmen between the sixteenth and the nineteenth centuries. It is true that his opening chapters
have little concern with Shakespeare, but their intrinsic interest and novelty atone for their irrele-
vance. They shed a flood of welcome light on that
interchange of literary information and ideas which
is a constant feature in the literary history of the
two countries.

Many will read here for the first time of the
great poet Ronsard's visits to this country; of the
distinguished company of English actors which de-
lighted the court of Henry IV. of France; and of
Ben Jonson's discreditable drunken exploits in the
French capital when he went thither as tutor to
Sir Walter Raleigh's son. To these episodes might
well be added the pleasant personal intercourse of
Francis Bacon's brother, Anthony, with the great
French essayist Montaigne, when the Englishman

was sojourning at Bordeaux in 1583. Montaigne's Essays achieved hardly less fame in Elizabethan England than in France. Both Shakespeare and Bacon gave proof of indebtedness to them.

By some freak of fortune Shakespeare's fame was slow in crossing the English Channel. The French dramatists of the sixteenth and seventeenth centuries lived and died in the paradoxical faith that the British drama reached its apogee in the achievement of the Scottish Latinist, George Buchanan, who was reckoned in France "prince of the poets of our day." In Buchanan's classical tragedies Montaigne played a part, while he was a student at Bordeaux. His tragedy of *Jephtha* achieved exceptional fame in sixteenth century France; three Frenchmen of literary repute rendered it independently into their own language, and each rendering went through several editions. Another delusion which French men of letters cherished not only during Shakespeare's lifetime but through three or four generations after his death, was that Sir Thomas More, Sir Philip Sidney, and the father of Lord Chancellor Bacon were the greatest authors which England had begotten or was likely to beget. French enthusiasm for the suggestive irony of More's Latin romance of *Utopia* outran that of his fellow-countrymen. A French translation anticipated the earliest rendering of the work in the author's native tongue. No less than two independent French versions of Sir Philip Sidney's voluminous fiction of *Arcadia* were circulating in France one hundred and twenty years before the like honour was paid to any work of Shakespeare.

Shakespeare's work first arrived in France tow-

ard the close of the seventeenth century. Frenchmen were staggered by its originality. They perceived the dramatist's colossal breaches of classical
law. They were shocked by his freedom of speech.
When Louis the Fourteenth's librarian placed on
the shelves of the Royal Library in Paris a copy of
the Second Folio of his works which had been published in London in 1632, he noted in his catalogue
that Shakespeare "has a rather fine imagination;
he thinks naturally; but these fine qualities are
obscured by the filth he introduces into his comedies." An increasing mass of pedestrian literature
was imported into France from England through
the middle and late years of the seventeenth century
Yet Shakespeare had to wait for a fair hearing ther
till the eighteenth century.

Then it was very gradually that Shakespeare's
pre-eminence was realised by French critics. It is
to Voltaire that Frenchmen owe a full knowledge
of Shakespeare. Voltaire's method of teaching
Shakespeare to his countrymen was characteristically
cynical. He studied him closely when he visited
England as a young man. At that period of his
career he not merely praised him with discerning
caution, but he paid him the flattery of imitation.
Voltaire's tragedy of *Brutus* betrays an intimate
acquaintance with Shakespeare's *Julius Cæsar*. His
Eryphile was the product of many perusals of *Hamlet*. His *Zaïre* is a pale reflection of *Othello*. But
when Voltaire's countrymen showed a tendency to
better Voltaire's instruction, and one Frenchman
conferred on Shakespeare the title of "the god of
the theatre," Voltaire resented the situation that he
had himself created. He was at the height of his

own fame, and he felt that his reputation as the first of French writers for the stage was in jeopardy.

The last years of Voltaire's life were therefore consecrated to an endeavour to dethrone the idol which his own hands had set up. Voltaire traded on the patriotic prejudices of his hearers, but his efforts to depreciate Shakespeare were very partially successful. Few writers of power were ready to second the soured critic,' and after Voltaire's death the Shakespeare cult in France, of which he was the unwilling inaugurator, spread far and wide.

In the nineteenth century Shakespeare was admitted without demur into the French "pantheon of literary gods." Classicists and romanticists vied in doing him honour. The classical painter Ingres introduced his portrait into his famous picture of "Homer's Cortège" (now in the Louvre). The romanticist Victor Hugo recognised only three men as memorable in the history of humanity, and Shakespeare was one of the three; Moses and Homer were the other two. Alfred de Musset became a dramatist under Shakespeare's spell. To George Sand everything in literature seemed tame by the side of Shakespeare's poetry. The prince of romancers, the elder Dumas, set the English dramatist next to God in the cosmic system; "After God," wrote Dumas, "Shakespeare has created most."

III

It would be easy to multiply eulogies of Shakespeare from French lips in the vein of Victor Hugo and Dumas—eulogies besides which the enthusiasm of many English critics appears cold and constrained. So unfaltering a note of admiration sounds gratefully in the ears of Shakespeare's countrymen. Yet on closer investigation there seems a rift within the lute. When one turns to the French versions of Shakespeare, for which the chief of Shakespeare's French encomiasts have made themselves responsible, an Englishman is inclined to moderate his exultation in the French panegyrics.

No one did more as an admiring critic and translator of Shakespeare than Jean François Ducis, who prepared six of Shakespeare's greatest plays for the French stage at the end of the eighteenth century. Not only did Ducis introduce Shakespeare's masterpieces to thousands of his countrymen who might otherwise never have heard of them, but his renderings of Shakespeare were turned into Italian and many languages of Eastern Europe. They spread the knowledge of Shakespeare's achievement to the extreme boundaries of the European Continent. Apparently Ducis did his work under favourable auspices. He corresponded regularly with Garrick, and he was never happier than when studying Shakespeare's text with a portrait of Shakespeare at his side. Yet, in spite of Ducis' unquestioned reverence and his honourable intentions, all his translations of Shakespeare are gross perversions of their originals. It is not merely that he is verbally unfaithful. He revises the development of the plots; he gives the *dramatis personæ* new names.

Ducis' *Othello* was accounted his greatest triumph. The play shows Shakespeare's mastery of the art of tragedy at its highest stage of development, and rewards the closest study. But the French translator ignored the great tragic conception which gives the drama its pith and movement. He converted the piece into a romance. Towards the end of his rendering Iago's villanies are discovered by Othello; Othello and Desdemona are reconciled; and the Moor, exulting in his newly recovered happiness, pardons Iago. The curtain falls on a dazzling scene of domestic bliss.

Ducis frankly acknowledged that he was guilty of a somewhat strained interpretation of Shakespeare's tragic scheme, but he defended himself on the ground that French refinement and French sensitiveness could not endure the agonising violence of the true catastrophe. It is, indeed, the fact that the patrons of the Comédie Française strictly warned the adapter against revolting their feelings by reproducing the "barbarities" that characterised the close of Shakespeare's tragic masterpiece.

If so fastidious a flinching from tragic episode breathe the true French sentiment, what, we are moved to ask, is the significance of the unqualified regard which Ducis and his countrymen profess for Shakespearean drama? There seems a strange paradox in the situation. The history of France proves that Frenchmen can face without quailing the direst tragedies which can be wrought in earnest off the stage. There is a startling inconsistency in the outcry of Ducis' French clients against the terror of Desdemona's murder. For the protests which Ducis reports on the part of the Parisians bear the date 1792. In that year the tragedy of the French Revolution—a tragedy of real life, grimmer than any that Shakespeare imagined—was being enacted in literal truth by the Parisian playgoers themselves. It would seem that Ducis and his country-

men deemed the purpose of art to be alone fulfilled
when the artistic fabric was divorced from the ugly
facts of life

A like problem is presented by Dumas' efforts
in more pacific conditions to adapt Shakespeare for
the Parisian stage. With his friend Paul Meurice
Dumas prepared the version of *Hamlet* which long
enjoyed a standard repute at the Comédie Française.
Dumas' ecstatic adoration for Shakespeare's genius
did not deter him, any more than Ducis was deterred
by his more subdued veneration, from working havoc
on the English text. Shakespeare's blank verse
was necessarily turned into Alexandrines. That was
comparatively immaterial. Of greater moment is
it to note that the *dénouement* of the tragedy was
completely revolutionised by Dumas. The tragic
climax is undermined. Hamlet's life is spared by
Dumas. The hero's dying exclamation, "The rest
is silence," disappears from Dumas' version. At
the close of the play the French translator makes
the ghost rejoin his son and good-naturedly promise
him indefinite prolongation of his earthly career.
According to the gospel of Dumas, the tragedy of
Hamlet ends, as soon as his and his father's wrongs
have been avenged, in this fashion:—

> *Hamlet.*   Et moi, vais-je rester, triste orphelin sur terre,
> A respirer cet air imprégné de misère? . . .
> Est-ce que Dieu sur moi fera peser son bras,
> Père? Et quel châtiment m'attend donc?
> *Le Fantôme.*   Tu vivras.

Such defiant transgressions of the true Shakespearean canon as those of which Ducis and Dumas
stand convicted may well rouse the suspicion that

the critical incense they burn at Shakespeare's shrine is offered with the tongue in the cheek. But that suspicion is not justified. Ducis and Dumas worship Shakespeare with a whole heart. Their misapprehensions of his tragic conceptions are due, involuntarily, to native temperament. In point of fact, Ducis and Dumas see Shakespeare through a distorting medium. The two Frenchmen were fully conscious of Shakespeare's towering greatness. They perceived intuitively that Shakespeare's tragedies transcended all other dramatic achievement. But their æsthetic sense, which, as far as the drama was concerned, was steeped in the classical spirit, set many of the essential features of Shakespeare's genius outside the focus of their vision.

To a Frenchman a tragedy of classical rank connotes "correctness," an absence of tumult, some observance of the classical law of unity of time, place, and action. The perpetration of crime in face of the audience outraged all classical conventions. Ducis and Dumas recognised involuntarily that certain characteristics of the Shakespearean drama could not live in the classical atmosphere of their own theatre. Excision, expansion, reduction was inevitable before Shakespeare could breathe the air of the French stage. The grotesque perversions of Ducis and Dumas were thus not the fruit of mere waywardness, or carelessness, or dishonesty; they admit of philosophical explanation.

By Englishmen they may be viewed with equanimity, if not with satisfaction. They offer strong proof of the irrepressible strength or catholicity of the appeal that Shakespeare's genius makes to the mind and heart of humanity. His spirit survived the French efforts at mutilation. The Gallicised or classicised contortions of his mighty work did not destroy its saving virtue. There is ground for congratulation that Ducis' and Dumas' perversions of Shakespeare excited among Frenchmen almost as devoted an homage as the dramatist's work in its native purity and perfection claims of men whose souls are free of the fetters of classical tradition.

IV

If any still doubt the sincerity of the worship which is offered Shakespeare in France, I would direct the sceptic's attention to a pathetically simple tribute which was paid to the dramatist by a French student in the first year of the last century, when England and France were in the grip of the Napoleonic War. It was then that a young Frenchman proved beyond cavil by an ingenuous confession that the English poet, in spite of the racial differences of æsthetic sentiment, could touch a French heart more deeply than any French or classical author. In 1801 there was published at Besançon, "de l'imprimerie de Métoyer," a very thin volume in small octavo, under fifty pages in length, entitled, *Pensées de Shakespeare, Extraites de ses Ouvrages*. No compiler's name is mentioned, but there is no doubt that the book was from the pen of a precocious native of Besançon, Charles Nodier, who was in later life to gain distinction as a bibliographer and writer of romance.

This forgotten volume, of which no more than twenty-five copies were printed, and only two or three of these seem to survive, has escaped the notice of M. Jusserand. No copy of it is in the British Museum, or in La Bibliothèque de l'Arsenal, with which the author, Nodier, was long honourably associated as librarian. I purchased it a few years ago by accident in a small collection of imperfectly catalogued Shakespeareana. Lurking in the rear of a very ragged regiment on the shelves of the auctioneer stood Charles Nodier's *Pensées de Shakespeare*. None competed with me for the prize. A very slight effort delivered into my hands the little chaplet of French laurel.

The major part of the volume consists of 190 numbered sentences—each a French rendering of an apophthegm or reflection drawn from Shakespeare's plays. The translator is not faithful to his English text, but his style is clear and often rises to eloquence. The book does not, however, owe its interest to Nodier's version of Shakespearean maxims. Nor can one grow enthusiastic over the dedication. "A elle"—an unidentified fair-one to whom the youthful writer proffers his homage with respectful propriety. The salt of the little volume lies in the "Observations Préliminaries," which cover less than five widely-printed pages. These observations breathe a genuine affection for Shakespeare's personality and a sense of gratitude for his achievement in terms which no English admirer has excelled for tenderness and simplicity.

"Shakespeare," writes this French worshipper, "is a friend whom Heaven has given to the unhappy of every age and every country." The writer warns us that he offers no eulogy of Shakespeare; that is to be found in the poet's works, which the

Frenchman for his own part prefers to read and read again rather than waste time in praising them. "The features of Alexander ought only to be preserved by Apelles." Nodier merely collects some of Shakespeare's thoughts on great moral truths which he thinks to be useful to the conduct of life. But such extracts, he admonishes his reader, supply no true knowledge of Shakespeare. " From Shakespeare's works one can draw forth a philosophy, but from no systems of philosophy could one construct one page of Shakespeare." Nodier concludes his "Observations" thus:—

"I advise those who do not know Shakespeare to study him in himself. I advise those who know him already to read him again. . . . I know him, but I must needs declare my admiration for him. I have reviewed my powers, and am content to cast a flower on his grave since I am not able to raise a monument to his memory."

Language like this admits no questioning of its sincerity. Nodier's modest tribute handsomely atones for his countrymen's misapprehensions of Shakespeare's tragic conceptions. None has phrased more delicately or more simply the sense of personal devotion, which is roused by close study of his work.

XI

THE COMMEMORATION OF SHAKE-SPEARE IN LONDON [1]

I

THE public memory is short. At the instant the suggestion that Shakespeare should receive the tribute of a great national monument in London is attracting general attention. In the ears of the vast majority of those who are taking part in the discussion the proposal appears to strike a new note. Few seem aware that a national memorial of Shakespeare has been urged on Londoners many times before. Thrice, at least, during the past eighty-five years has it exercised the public mind.

At the extreme end of the year 1820, the well-known actor, Charles Mathews, set on foot a movement for the erection of "a national monument to the immortal memory of Shakespeare." He pledged himself to enlist the support of the new King, George the Fourth, of members of the royal family, of "every man of rank and talent, every poet, artist, and sculptor." Mathews' endeavour achieved

[1] This paper was first printed in *The Nineteenth Century and After*, April, 1905.

only a specious success. George the Fourth readily
gave his "high sanction" to a London memorial.
Sir Walter Scott, Samuel Taylor Coleridge, Tom
Moore, and Washington Irving were among the men
of letters; Sir Thomas Lawrence, [Sir] Francis Chan-
trey, and John Nash, the architect, were among the
artists, who approved the general conception. For
three or four years ink was spilt and breath was
spent in the advocacy of the scheme. But nothing
came of all the letters and speeches.

In 1847 the topic was again broached. A committee, which was hardly less influential than that
of 1821, revived the proposal. Again no result
followed.

Seventeen years passed away, and then, in 1864,
the arrival of the tercentenary of Shakespeare's
birth seemed to many men of eminence in public life,
in letters or in art, an appropriate moment at which
to carry the design into effect. A third failure has
to be recorded.

The notion, indeed, was no child of the nineteenth century which fathered it so ineffectually.
It was familiar to the eighteenth. One eighteenth-
century effort was fortunate enough to yield a little
permanent fruit. To an eighteenth-century endeavour to offer Shakespeare a national memorial in
London was due the cenotaph in Westminster Abbey.

II

The suggestion of commemorating Shakespeare
by means of a monument in London has thus something more than a "smack of age" about it, something more than a "relish of the saltness of time";

there are points of view from which it might appear
to be already "blasted with antiquity." On only
one of the previous occasions that the question was
raised was the stage of discussion passed, and that
was in the eighteenth century when the monument
was placed in the Poets' Corner of Westminster
Abbey. The issue was not felicitous. The memorial
in the Abbey failed to satisfy the commemorative
aspirations of the nation; it left it open to succeeding generations to reconsider the question, if it did
not impose on them the obligation. Most of the
poets, actors, scholars, and patrons of polite learning, who in 1741 subscribed their guineas to the
fund for placing a monument in Westminster Abbey,
resented the sculpturesque caricature to which their
subscriptions were applied. Pope, an original leader
of the movement, declined to write an inscription for
this national memorial, but scribbled some ironical
verses beginning:—

Thus Britons love me and preserve my fame.

A later critic imagined Shakespeare's wraith pausing
in horror by the familiar monument in the Abbey,
and lightly misquoting Shelley's familiar lines:—

I silently laugh at my own cenotaph, . . .
And long to unbuild it again.

One of the most regrettable effects of the Abbey
memorial, with its mawkish and irrelevant sentimentality, has been to set a bad pattern for statues of
Shakespeare. Posterity came to invest the design
with some measure of sanctity.

The nineteenth-century efforts were mere abor-
tions. In 1821, in spite of George the Fourth's
benevolent patronage, which included an unfulfilled

promise to pay the sum of 100 guineas, the total amount which was collected after six years' agitation was so small that it was returned to the subscribers. The accounts are extant in the Library of Shakespeare's Birthplace at Stratford-on-Avon. In 1847 the subscriptions were more abundant, but all was then absorbed in the purchase of Shakespeare's Birthplace at Stratford; no money was available for a London memorial. In 1864 the expenses of organising the tercentenary celebration in London by way of banquets, concerts, and theatrical performances, seem to have left no surplus for the purpose which the movement set out to fulfil.

III

The causes of the sweeping failure of the proposal when it came before the public during the nineteenth century are worthy of study. There was no lack of enthusiasm among the promoters. Nor were their high hopes wrecked solely by public apathy. The public interest was never altogether dormant. More efficient causes of ruin were, firstly, the active hostility of some prominent writers and actors who declaimed against all outward and visible commemoration of Shakespeare; and secondly, divisions in the ranks of supporters in regard to the precise form that the memorial ought to take. The censorious refusal of one section of the literary public to countenance any memorial at all, and the inability of another section, while promoting the endeavour, to concentrate its energies on a single acceptable form of commemoration had, as might be expected, a paralysing effect.

"England," it was somewhat casuistically argued

in 1864, "has never been ungrateful to her poet; but the very depth and fervour of the reverence in which he is held have hitherto made it difficult for his scholars to agree upon any common proceeding in his name." Neither in 1864 nor at earlier and later epochs have Shakespearean scholars always formed among themselves a very happy family. That amiable sentiment which would treat the realisation of the commemorative aim as a patriotic obligation —as an obligation which no good citizen could honourably repudiate—has often produced discord rather than harmony among the Shakespearean scholars who cherish it. One school of these has argued in the past for a work of sculpture, and has been opposed by a cry for a college for actors, or a Shakespearean theatre. "We do not like the idea of a monument at all," wrote *The Times* on the 20th of January 1864. "Shakespeare," wrote *Punch* on the 6th of February following, "needs no statue." In old days it was frequently insisted that, even if the erection of a London monument were desirable, active effort ought to be postponed until an adequate memorial had been placed in Stratford-on-Avon where the poet's memory had been hitherto inadequately honoured. At the same time a band of students was always prepared to urge the chilling plea that the payment of any outward honour to Shakespeare was laboursome futility, was "wasteful and ridiculous excess." Milton's query: "What needs my Shakespeare for his honoured bones?" has always been quoted to satiety by a vociferous section of the critics whenever the commemoration of Shakespeare has come under discussion.

IV

Once again the question of a national memorial of Shakespeare in London has been revived in conditions not wholly unlike those that have gone before. Mr Richard Badger, a veteran enthusiast for Shakespeare, who was educated in the poet's native place, has offered the people of London the sum of £3500 as the nucleus of a great Shakespeare Memorial Fund. The Lord Mayor of London has presided over a public meeting at the Mansion House, which has empowered an influential committee to proceed with the work. The London County Council has promised to provide a site. With regard to the form that the memorial ought to take, a variety of irresponsible suggestions has been made. It has now been authoritatively determined to erect a sculptured monument on the banks of the Thames.[1]

The propriety of visibly and outwardly commemorating Shakespeare in the capital city of the Empire has consequently become once more an urgent public question. The public is invited anew to form an opinion on the various points at issue. No expression of opinion should carry weight which omits to take into account past experience as well as present conditions and possibilities. If regard for

[1] The proceedings of the committee which was formed in the spring of 1905 have been dilatory. Mr Badger informs me that he paid the organisers, nearly two years ago, the sum of £500 for preliminary expenses, and deposited bonds to the value of £3,000 with Lord Avebury, the treasurer of the committee. The delay is assigned to the circumstance that the London County Council, which is supporting the proposal, is desirous of associating it with the great Council Hall which it is preparing to erect on the south side of the Thames, and that it has not yet been found practicable to invite designs for that work (Oct. 1, 1906).

the public interest justify a national memorial in London, it is most desirable to define the principles whereby its precise form should be determined.

In one important particular the consideration of the subject to-day is simpler than when it was debated on former occasions. Differences existed, then as now, in regard to the propriety of erecting a national memorial of Shakespeare in London; but almost all who interested themselves in the matter in the nineteenth century agreed that the public interest justified, if it did not require, the preservation from decay or demolition of the buildings at Stratford-on-Avon with which Shakespeare's life was associated. So long as those buildings were in private hands, every proposal to commemorate Shakespeare in London had to meet a formidable objection which was raised on their behalf. If the nation undertook to commemorate Shakespeare at all, it should make its first aim (it was argued) the conversion into public property of the surviving memorials of Shakespeare's career at Stratford. The scheme of the London memorial could not be thoroughly discussed on its merits while the claims of Stratford remained unsatisfied. It was deemed premature, whether or no it were justifiable, to entertain any scheme of commemoration which left the Stratford buildings out of account.

A natural sentiment connected Shakespeare more closely with Stratford-on-Avon than with any other place. Whatever part London played in his career, the public mind was dominated by the fact that he was born at Stratford, died, and was buried there. If he left Stratford in youth in order to work out his destiny in London, he returned to it in middle life in order to end his days there "in ease, retirement, and the conversation of his friends."

In spite of this widespread feeling, it proved no easy task, nor one capable of rapid fulfilment, to consecrate in permanence to public uses the extant memorials of Shakespeare at Stratford-on-Avon. Stratford was a place of pilgrimage for admirers of Shakespeare from early days in the seventeenth century—soon, in fact, after Shakspeare's death in 1616. But local veneration did not prevent the demolition in 1759, by a private owner, of New Place, Shakespeare's last residence. That act of vandalism was long in provoking any effective resentment. Garrick, by means of his Jubilee Festival of 1769, effectively, if somewhat theatrically, called the attention of the English public to the claims of the town to the affectionate regard of lovers of the great dramatist. Nevertheless, it was left to the nineteenth century to dedicate in perpetuity to the public service the places which were the scenes of Shakespeare's private life in his native town.

Charles Mathews' effort of 1821 took its rise in an endeavour to purchase in behalf of the nation the vacant site of Shakespeare's demolished residence of New Place, with the great garden attached to it. But that scheme was overweighted by the incorporation with it of the plan for a London monument, and both collapsed ignominiously. In 1835 a strong committee was formed at Stratford to commemorate the poet's connection with the town. It was called "the Monumental Committee," and had for its object, firstly, the repair of Shakespeare's tomb in the Parish Church; and secondly, the preservation and restoration of all the Shakespearean buildings in the town. Subscriptions were limited to £1, and all the members of the royal family, including the Princess Victoria, who two years later came to the throne, figured, with other leading personages in the nation's life, in the list of subscribers. But the subscriptions only produced a sum sufficient to carry out the first purpose of the Monumental Committee— the repair of the tomb.

In 1847 the sale by public auction was announced of the house in which Shakespeare was born. It had long been a show-place in private hands. A general feeling declared itself in favour of the purchase of the house for the nation. Public sentiment was in accord with the ungrammatical grandiloquence of the auctioneer, the famous Robins, whose advertisement of the sale included the sentence: "It is trusted the feeling of the country will be so evinced that the structure may be secured, hallowed and cherished as a national monument almost as imperishable as the poet's fame." A subscription list was headed by Prince Albert with £250. A distinguished committee was formed under the presidency of Lord Morpeth (afterwards the seventh Earl of Carlisle), then Chief Commissioner of Woods and Forests, who offered to make his department perpetual conservators of the property. (That proposal was not accepted.) Dickens, Macaulay, Lord Lytton, and the historian Grote were all active in promoting the movement, and it proved successful. The property was duly secured by a private trust in behalf of the nation. The most important house identified with Shakespeare's career in Stratford was thus effectively protected from the risks that are always inherent in private ownership. The step was not taken with undue haste; two hundred and thirty-one years had elapsed since Shakespeare's death.

Fourteen years later, in very similar circumstances, the still vacant site of Shakespeare's demolished residence, New Place, with the great garden behind it, and the adjoining house, were acquired by the public. A new Shakespeare Fund, to which the Prince Consort subscribed £100, and Miss Burdett-Coutts (afterwards Baroness Burdett-Coutts) £600, was formed not only to satisfy this purpose, but to provide the means of equipping a library and museum which were contemplated at the Birthplace, as well as a second museum which was to be provided on the New Place property. It was appropriate to make these buildings depositories of authentic relics and books which should illustrate the poet's life and work. This national Shakespeare Fund was actively promoted, chiefly by the late Mr Halliwell-Phillipps, for more than ten years; a large sum of money was collected, and the aims with which the Fund was set on foot were to a large extent fulfilled. It only remained to organise on a permanent legal basis the completed Stratford Memorial of Shakespeare. By an Act of Parliament passed in 1891 the two properties of New Place and the Birthplace were definitely formed into a single public trust "for and in behalf of the nation." The trustees were able in 1892, out of their surplus income, which is derived from the fees of visitors, to add to their estates Anne Hathaway's Cottage at Shottery, a third building of high interest to students of Shakespeare's history.

The formation of the Birthplace Trust has every title to be regarded as an outward and visible tribute to Shakespeare's memory on the part of the British

nation at large.[1]   The purchase for the public of the
Birthplace, the New Place property, and Anne
Hathaway's Cottage was not primarily due to local
effort.   Justly enough, a very small portion of the
necessary funds came from Stratford itself.   The
British nation may therefore take credit for having
set up at least one fitting monument to Shakespeare
by consecrating to public uses the property identified
with his career in Stratford.   Larger funds than
the trustees at present possess are required to enable
them to carry on the work which their predecessors
began, and to compete with any chance of success
for books and relics of Shakespearean interest—
such as they are empowered by Act of Parliament
to acquire—when these memorials chance to come
into the market.   But a number of small annual
subscriptions from men of letters has lately facilitated
the performance of this part of the trustees' work,
and that source of income may, it is hoped, increase.

At any rate, the ancient objection to the erection

[1] Nor is this all that has been accomplished at Stratford in the
nineteenth century in the way of the national commemoration of
Shakespeare.   While the surviving property of Shakespearean
interest was in course of acquisition for the nation, an early ambition to erect in Stratford a theatre in Shakespeare's memory
was realised—in part by subscriptions from the general public,
but mainly by the munificence of members of the Flower family,
three generations of which have resided at Stratford.   The
Memorial Theatre was opened in 1879, and the Picture Gallery
and Library which were attached to it were completed two years
later.   The Memorial Buildings at Stratford stand on a different
footing from the properties of the Birthplace Trust.   The Memorial institution has an independent government, and is to a larger
extent under local control.   But the extended series of performances of Shakespearean drama, which takes place each year in
April at the Memorial Theatre, has something of the character
of an annual commemoration of Shakespeare by the nation at
large.

of a national monument in London, which was based on the absence of any memorial in Stratford, is no longer of avail. In 1821, in 1847, and in 1864, when the acquisition of the Stratford property was unattempted or uncompleted, it was perfectly just to argue that Stratford was entitled to have precedence of London when the question of commemorating Shakespeare was debated. It is no just argument in 1906, now that the claims of Stratford are practically satisfied.

Byron, when writing of the memorial to Petrarch at Arquà, expressed with admirable feeling the sentiment that would confine outward memorials of a poet in his native town to the places where he was born, lived, died, and was buried. With very little verbal change Byron's stanza on the visible memorials of Petrarch's association with Arquà is applicable to those of Shakespeare's connexion with Stratford :—

> They keep his dust in Stratford, where he died;
> The midland village where his later days
> Went down the vale of years; and 'tis their pride—
> An honest pride—and let it be their praise,
> To offer to the passing stranger's gaze
> His birthplace and his sepulchre; both plain
> And venerably simple, such as raise
> A feeling more accordant with his strain
> Than if a pyramid form'd his monumental fane.[1]

Venerable simplicity is hardly the characteristic note of Shakespeare's "strain" any more than it is of Petrarch's "strain." But there can be no just quarrel with the general contention that at Stratford, where Shakespeare gave ample proof of his characteristic modesty, a pyramidal fane would be out of harmony with the environment. There his

[1] Cf. *Childe Harold*, Canto IV., St. xxxi.

birthplace, his garden, and tomb are the fittest
memorials of his great career.

V

It may justly be asked: Is there any principle
which justifies another sort of memorial elsewhere?
On grounds of history and sentiment, but in conditions which demand most careful definition, the
right answer will, I think, be in the affirmative. For
one thing, Shakespeare's life was not confined to
Stratford. His professional career was spent in
London, and those, who strictly insist that memorials
to great men should be erected only in places with
which they were personally associated, can hardly
deny that London shares with Stratford a title to
a memorial from a biographical or historical point
of view. Of Shakespeare's life of fifty-two years,
twenty-four years were in all probability spent in
London. During those years the work that makes
him memorable was done. It was in London that
the fame which is universally acknowledged was
won.

Some valuable details regarding Shakespeare's
life in London are accessible. The districts where he
resided and where he passed his days are known.
There is evidence that during the early part of his
London career he lived in the parish of St Helen's,
Bishopsgate, and during the later part near the Bankside, Southwark. With the south side of the Thames
he was long connected, together with his youngest
brother, Edmund, who was also an actor, and who
was buried in the church of St Saviour's, Southwark.

In his early London days Shakespeare's professional work, alike as actor and dramatist, brought him daily from St Helen's, Bishopsgate, to The Theatre in Shoreditch. Shoreditch was then the chief theatrical quarter in London. Later, the centre of London theatrical life shifted to Southwark, where the far-famed Globe Theatre was erected, in 1599, mainly out of the materials of the dismantled Shoreditch Theatre. Ultimately Shakespeare's company of actors performed in a theatre at Blackfriars, which was created out of a private residence on a part of the site on which *The Times* office stands now. At a few hundred yards' distance from the Blackfriars Theatre, in the direction of Cannon Street, Shakespeare, too, shortly before his death, purchased a house.

Thus Shakespeare's life in London is well identified with four districts — with Bishopsgate, with Shoreditch, with Southwark, and with Blackfriars. Unhappily for students of Shakespeare's life, London has been more than once remodelled since the dramatist sojourned in the city. The buildings and lodgings, with which he was associated in Shoreditch, Southwark, Bishopsgate, or Blackfriars, have long since disappeared.

It is not practicable to follow in London the same historical scheme of commemoration which has been adopted at Stratford-on-Avon. It is impossible to recall to existence the edifices in which Shakespeare pursued his London career. Archæology could do little in this direction that was satisfactory. There would be an awkward incongruity in introducing into the serried ranks of Shoreditch warehouses and Southwark wharves an archæological restoration of Elizabethan playhouse or private residence. Pictorial

representations of the Globe Theatre survive, and
it might be possible to construct something that
should materialise the extant drawings. But the
genius loci has fled from Southwark and from Shoreditch. It might be practicable to set up a new
model of an Elizabethan theatre elsewhere in London,
but such a memorial would have about it an air of
unreality, artificiality, and affectation which would
not be in accord with the scholarly spirit of an historic or biographic commemoration. The device
might prove of archæological interest, but the commemorative purpose, from a biographical or historical point of view, would be ill served. Wherever
a copy of an Elizabethan playhouse were brought
to birth in twentieth-century London, the historic
sense in the onlooker would be for the most part
irresponsive; it would hardly be quickened.

VI

Apart from the practical difficulties of realising
materially Shakespeare's local associations with London, it is doubtful if the mere commemoration in
London of Shakespeare's personal connexion with
the great city ought to be the precise aim of those
who urge the propriety of erecting a national monument in the metropolis. Shakespeare's personal relations with London can in all the circumstances of
the case be treated as a justification in only the second
degree. The primary justification involves a somewhat different train of thought. A national memorial
of Shakespeare in London must be reckoned of small
account if it merely aim at keeping alive in public

memory episodes of Shakespeare's London career. The true aim of a national London memorial must be symbolical of a larger fact. It must typify Shakespeare's place not in the past, but in the present life of the nation and of the world. It ought to constitute a perpetual reminder of the position that he fills in the present economy, and is likely to fill in the future economy of human thought, for those whose growing absorption in the narrowing business of life tends to make them forget it.

The day is long since past when vague eulogy of Shakespeare is permissible. Shakespeare's literary supremacy is as fully recognised by those who justly appreciate literature as any law of nature. To the man and woman of culture in all civilised countries he symbolises the potency of the human intellect. But those who are content to read and admire him in the cloister at times overlook the full significance of his achievement in the outer world. Critics of all nationalities are in substantial agreement with the romance-writer Dumas, who pointed out that Shakespeare is more than the greatest of dramatists; he is the greatest of thinking men.

The exalted foreign estimate illustrates the fact that Shakespeare contributes to the prestige of his nation a good deal beyond repute for literary power. He is not merely a literary ornament of our British household. It is largely on his account that foreign nations honour his country as an intellectual and spiritual force. Shakespeare and Newton together give England an intellectual sovereignty which adds more to her "reputation through the world" than any exploit in battle or statesmanship. If, again, Shakespeare's pre-eminence has added dignity to the

name of Englishman abroad, it has also quickened
the sense of unity among the intelligent sections of
the English-speaking peoples. Admiration, affection for his work has come to be one of the strongest
links in the chain which binds the English-speaking
peoples together. He quickens the fraternal sense
among all who speak his language.

London is no nominal capital of the kingdom and
the Empire. It is the headquarters of British influence. Within its boundaries are assembled the
official insignia of British prestige. It is the mother-
city of the English-speaking world. To ask of the
citizens of London some outward sign that Shakespeare is a living source of British prestige, an unify-
ing factor in the consolidation of the British Empire,
and a powerful element in the maintenance of fraternal relations with the United States, seems therefore
no unreasonable demand. Neither cloistered study
of his plays, nor the occasional representation of
them in the theatres, brings home to either the
English-speaking or the English-reading world the
full extent of the debt that England owes to Shakespeare. A monumental memorial, which should
symbolise Shakespeare's influence in the universe,
could only find an appropriate and effective home in
the capital city of the British Empire. It is this
conviction, and no narrower point of view, which
gives endeavour to commemorate Shakespeare in
London its title to consideration.

VII

The admitted fact that Shakespeare's fame is
established beyond risk of decay does not place him

outside the range of conventional methods of commemoration. The greater a man's recognised service to his fellows, the more active grows in normally
constituted minds that natural commemorative instinct, which seeks outward and tangible expression.
A strange fallacy underlies the objection that has
been taken to any commemoration of Shakespeare
on the alleged ground that Milton warned the English
people of all time against erecting a monument to
Shakespeare.

In 1630 Milton asked the question that is familiar
to thousands of tongues:

What needs my Shakespeare for his honoured bones?

By way of answer he deprecated any such "weak
witness of his name" as "piléd stones" or "star-y-
pointing pyramid." The poet-laureate of England
echoed Milton's sentiment in 1905. He roundly
asserted that "perishable stuff" is the fit crown of
monumental pedestals. "Gods for themselves," he
concluded, "have monument enough."

There are ample signs that the sentiment to
which Milton and the laureate give voice has a good
deal of public support. None the less the poet-
laureate's conclusion is clearly refuted by experience
and cannot terminate the argument. At any rate,
in the classical and Renaissance eras monumental
sculpture was in habitual request among those who
would honour both immortal gods and mortal heroes
—especially mortal heroes who had distinguished
themselves in literature or art.

A little reflection will show, likewise, that Milton's
fervid couplets have small bearing on the question
at issue in its present conditions. Milton's poem

is an elegy on Shakespeare. It was penned when
the dramatist had lain in his grave less than fourteen
years, and when the writer was in his twenty-second
year. The exuberant enthusiasm of youth was
couched in poetic imagery which has from time
immemorial been employed in panegyrics of great
poets. The beautiful figure which presents a great
man's work as his only lasting monument is as
old as poetry itself. The conceit courses through
the classical poetry of Greece from the time of
Pindar, and through that of Italy from the time
of Ennius. No great Renaissance writer of modern
Italy, of sixteenth-century France, or of Elizabethan
England, tired of arguing that the poet's deathless
memorial is that carved by his own pen. Shakespeare himself clothed the conceit in glowing har-
monies in his sonnets. Ben Jonson, in his elegy on
the dramatist, adapted the time-honoured figure
when he hailed his dead friend's achievement as "a
monument without a tomb."

"The truest poetry is the most feigning," and,
when one recalls the true significance and influence
of great sculptured monuments through the history
of the civilised world, Milton's poetic argument
can only be accepted in what Sir Thomas Browne
called "a soft and flexible sense"; it cannot "be
called unto the rigid test of reason." To treat
Milton's eulogy as the final word in the discussion
of the subject whether or no Shakespeare should
have a national monument, is to come into conflict
with Sir Walter Scott, Tennyson, Ruskin, Dickens,
and all the greatest men of letters of the nineteenth
century, who answered the question in the affirmative. It is to discredit crowds of admirers of grea'

writers in classical and modern ages, who have commemorated the labours of poets and dramatists in
outward and visible monuments.

The genius of the great Greek dramatists was
not underrated by their countrymen. Their literary
efforts were adjudged to be true memorials of their
fame, and no doubt of their immortality was entertained. None the less, the city of Athens, on the
proposition of the Attic orator, Lycurgus, erected in
honour of Æschylus, Sophocles, and Euripides statues
which ranked with the most beautiful adornments
of the Greek capital. Calderon and Goethe, Camo-
ens and Schiller, Sir Walter Scott and Burns enjoy
reputations which are smaller, it is true, than
Shakespeare's, but are, at the same time, like his,
of both national and universal significance. In
memory of them all, monuments have been erected
as tokens of their fellow-countrymen's veneration
and gratitude for the influence which their poetry
wields.

The fame of these men's writings never stood
in any "need" of monumental corroboration. The
sculptured memorial testified to the sense of gratitude
which their writings generated in the hearts and
minds of their readers.

Again, the great musicians and the great painters
live in their work in a singularly vivid sense. Music
and painting are more direct in popular appeal than
great poetry. Yet none can ridicule the sentiment
which is embodied in the statue of Beethoven at
Bonn, or in that of Paolo Veronese at Verona. To
accept literally the youthful judgment of Milton and
his imitators is to condemn sentiments and practices
which are in universal vogue among civilised peoples.

It is to deny to the Poets' Corner in Westminster Abbey a rational title to existence.

To commemorate a great man by a statue in a public place in the central sphere of his influence is, indeed, a custom inseparable from civilised life. The theoretic moralist's reminder that monuments of human greatness sooner or later come to dust is a doctrine too discouraging of all human effort to exert much practical effect. Monuments are, in the eyes of the intelligent, tributes for services rendered by great men to posterity. But incidentally they have an educational value. They help to fix the attention of the thoughtless on facts which may, in the absence of outward symbols, escape notice. They may act as incentives to thought. They may convert the thoughtless into the thoughtful. Wide as are the ranks of Shakespeare's readers, they are not, in England at any rate, incapable of extension; and, whatever is likely to call the attention of those who are as yet outside the pale of knowledge of Shakespeare to what lies within it, deserves respectful consideration.

It is never inconsistent with a nation's dignity for it to give conspicuous expression of gratitude to its benefactors, among whom great writers take first rank. Monuments of fitting character give that conspicuous expression. Bacon, the most enlightened of English thinkers, argued, within a few years of Shakespeare's death, that no self-respecting people could safely omit to erect statues of those who had contributed to the genuine advance of their knowledge or prestige. The visitors to Bacon's imaginary island of New Atlantis saw statues erected at the public expense in memory

of all who had won great distinction in the arts
or sciences. The richness of the memorial varied
according to the value of the achievement. "These
statues," the observer noted, "are some of brass,
some of marble and touchstone, some of cedar
and other special woods, gilt and adorned, some
of iron, some of silver, some of gold." No other
external recognition of great intellectual service was
deemed, in Bacon's Utopia, of equal appropriateness.
Bacon's mature judgment deserves greater regard
than the splendid imagery of Milton's budding
muse.

VIII

In order to satisfy the commemorative instinct
in a people, it is necessary, as Bacon pointed out,
strictly to adapt the means to the end. The essential
object of a national monument to a great man is
to pay tribute to his greatness, to express his fellow-
men's sense of his service. No blunder could be
graver than to confuse the issue by seeking to make
the commemoration serve any secondary or collateral
purpose. It may be very useful to erect hospitals
or schools. It may help in the dissemination of
knowledge and appreciation of Shakespearean drama
for the public to endow a theatre, which should be
devoted to the performance of Shakespeare's plays.
The public interest calls loudly for a playhouse that
shall be under public control. Promoters of such
a commendable endeavour might find their labours
facilitated by associating their project with Shakespeare's name—with the proposed commemoration
of Shakespeare. But the true aim of the commemoration will be frustrated if it be linked with

any purpose of utility, however commendable, with anything beyond a symbolisation of Shakespeare's mighty genius and influence. To attempt aught else is "wrenching the true cause the false way." A worthy memorial to Shakespeare will not satisfy the just working of the commemorative instinct, unless it take the sculpturesque and monumental shape which the great tradition of antiquity has sanctioned. A monument to Shakespeare should be a monument and nothing besides.

Bacon's doctrine that the greater the achievement that is commemorated the richer must be the outward symbol, implies that a memorial to Shakespeare must be a work of art of the loftiest merit conceivable. Unless those who promote the movement concentrate their energies on an object of beauty, unless they free the movement of all suspicion that the satisfaction of the commemorative instinct is to be a secondary and not the primary aim, unless they resolve that the Shakespeare memorial in London is to be a monument pure and simple, and one as perfect as art can make it, then the effort is undeserving of national support.

IX

This conclusion suggests the inevitable objection that sculpture in England is not in a condition favourable to the execution of a great piece of monumental art. Past experience in London does not make one very sanguine that it is possible to realise in statuary a worthy conception of a Shakespearean memorial. The various stages through which recent efforts to promote sculptured memorials in London have passed suggest the mock turtle's definition in *Alice in Wonderland* of the four branches of arithmetic—Ambition, Distraction, Uglification, and Derision. Save the old statue of James the Second, at Whitehall, and the new statue of Oliver Cromwell, which stands at a disadvantage on its present site beneath Westminster Hall, there is scarcely a sculptured portrait in the public places of London which is not

> A fixèd figure for the time of scorn
> To point his slow unmoving finger at.

London does not lack statues of men of letters. There are statues of Burns and John Stuart Mill on the Thames Embankment, of Byron in Hamilton Place, and of Carlyle on Chelsea Embankment. But all convey an impression of insignificance, and thereby fail to satisfy the nation's commemorative instinct.

The taste of the British nation needs rigorous control when it seeks to pay tribute to benefactors by means of sculptured monuments. During the last forty years a vast addition has been made throughout Great Britain—with most depressing effect—to the number of sculptured memorials in the open air. The people have certainly shown far too enthusiastic and too inconsiderate a liberality in commemorating by means of sculptured monuments the virtues of Prince Albert and the noble character and career of the late Queen Victoria. The deduction to be drawn from the numberless statues of Queen Victoria and her consort is not exhilarating. British taste never showed itself to worse effect. The general impression produced by the most ambitious of all these memorials, the Albert Memorial in Kensington Gardens, is especially deplorable. The gilt figure of

the Prince seems to defy every principle that fine art
should respect.   The endeavour to produce imposing
effect by dint of hugeness is, in all but inspired hands,
certain to issue in ugliness.

It would, however, be a mistake to take too
gloomy a view of the situation.   The prospect may
easily be painted in too dismal colours.   It is a commonplace with foreign historians of art to assert that
English sculpture ceased to flourish when the building of the old Gothic cathedrals came to an end.
But Stevens's monument of the Duke of Wellington
in St. Paul's Cathedral, despite the imperfect execution of the sculptor's design, shows that the monumental art of England has proved itself, at a recent
date, capable of realising a great commemorative
conception.   There are signs, too, that at least three
living sculptors might in favourable conditions prove
worthy competitors of Stevens.   At least one literary
memorial in the British Isles, the Scott monument
in Edinburgh, which cost no more than £16,000,
satisfies   a   nation's   commemorative   aspiration.
There the natural environment and an architectural
setting of fine conception reinforce the effect of sculpture.   The whole typifies with fitting dignity the
admiring affection which gathers about Scott's name.
This successful realisation of a commemorative aim—
not wholly dissimilar from that which should inspire
a Shakespeare memorial—must check forebodings of
despair.

There are obviously greater difficulties in erecting
a monument to Shakespeare in London than in
erecting a monument to Scott in Edinburgh.   There
is no site in London that will compare with the
gardens of Princes Street in Edinburgh.   It is

essential that a Shakespeare memorial should occupy the best site that London can offer. Ideally
the best site for any great monument is the summit
of a gently rising eminence, with a roadway directly
approaching it and circling round it. In 1864,
when the question of a fit site for a Shakespeare
memorial in London was warmly debated, a too
ambitious scheme recommended the formation of
an avenue on the model of the Champs-Elysées
from the top of Portland Place across Primrose
Hill; and at the end of the avenue, on the summit
of Primrose Hill, at an elevation of 207 feet above
the river Thames, the Shakespeare monument was
to stand. This was and is an impracticable proposal.
The site which in 1864 received the largest measure
of approbation was a spot in the Green Park, near
Piccadilly. A third suggestion of the same date was
the bank of the river Thames, which was then called
Thamesway, but was on the point of conversion into
the Thames Embankment. Recent reconstruction
of Central London—of the district north of the
Strand—by the London County Council now widens
the field of choice. There is much to be said for a
site within the centre of London life. But an ele-
vated monumental structure on the banks of the
Thames seems to meet at the moment with the wid-
est approval. In any case, no site that is mean or
cramped would be permissible if the essential needs
of the situation are to be met.

A monument that should be sufficiently imposing
would need an architectural framework. But the
figure of the poet must occupy the foremost place
in the design. Herein lies another embarrassment.
It is difficult to determine which of the extant

portraits the sculptor ought to follow. The bust
in Stratford Church, the print in the First Folio,
and possibly the Chandos painting in the National
Portrait Gallery, are honest efforts to present a
faithful likeness. But they are crudely executed,
and are posthumous sketches largely depending
on the artist's memory. The sculptor would be
compelled to work in the spirit of the historian,
who recreates a past event from the indication
given him by an illiterate or fragmentary chronicle
or inscription. He would be bound to endow with
artistic life those features in which the authentic
portraits agree, but the highest effort of the imagination would be needed to create an impression of
artistic truth.

The success of a Shakespeare memorial will
ultimately depend on the pecuniary support that
the public accord it. But in the initial stage of
the movement all rests on the discovery of a sculptor
capable of realising the significance of a national
commemoration of the greatest of the nation's, or
indeed of the world's, heroes. It would be well to
settle satisfactorily the question of such an artist's existence before anything else. The first step
that any organising committee of a Shakespeare
memorial should therefore take, in my view, would
be to invite sculptors of every country to propose
a design. The monument should be the best that
artistic genius could contrive—the artistic genius
of the world. There may be better sculptors
abroad than at home. The universality of the appeal which Shakespeare's achievement makes, justifies a competition among artists of every race or
nationality.

The crucial decision as to whether the capacity to execute the monument is available, should be entrusted to a committee of taste, to a committee of liberal-minded connoisseurs who command general confidence. If this jury decide by their verdict that the present conditions of art permit the production of a great memorial of Shakespeare on just principles, then a strenuous appeal for funds may be inaugurated with likelihood of success. It is hopeless to reverse these methods of procedure. If funds are first invited before rational doubts as to the possibility of a proper application of them are dispelled, it is improbable that the response will be satisfactory or that the issue of the movement of 1905 will differ from that of 1821 or 1864.

In 1864 Victor Hugo expressed the opinion that the expenses of a Shakespeare memorial in London ought to be defrayed by the British Government. There is small likelihood of assistance from that source. Individual effort can alone be relied upon; and it is doubtful if it be desirable to seek official aid. A great national memorial of Shakespeare in London, if it come into being at all on the lines which would alone justify its existence, ought to embody individual enthusiasm, ought to express with fitting dignity the personal sense of indebtedness and admiration which fills the hearts of his fellow-men.

INDEX

INDEX

Acting, importance of, in Shakespearean drama, 13; evil effects of long runs, 14; Shakespeare on, 45, 47.

Actor-manager, his merits and defects, 125, 126.

Actors, training of, 139; English, in France, 203. See also *Benson, Mr. F. R.*, and *Boys*.

Æschylus, statue of, 233.

Albert, Prince (consort), and Shakespeare's birthplace, 222; statues of, 237, 238.

Alleyn, Edward, 191, 194.

Annual Register of 1770, 194.

Aristotle, Shakespeare's mention of, 144, 145; Bacon's study of, 145.

Arnold, Matthew, on Shakespeare, 29.

Astronomy, Shakespeare on, 146.

Athens, statuary at, 233.

Aubrey, John, his gossip of Shakespeare, 66, 67.

Austria, subsidised theatres in, 131, 136.

Bacon, Anthony, in France, 203.

Bacon, Francis, philosophical method of, 143; on memorial monuments in *New Atlantis*, 234, 235.

Bacon, Sir Nicholas, his fame in France, 204.

Badger, Mr. Richard, proposal for a Shakespeare monument, 219.

Bannister, music for *The Tempest*, 106, 107.

Barker, Mr. Granville, as Richard II., 13 *n*.

Basse, William, his tribute to Shakespeare, 50.

Beeston, Christopher, Elizabethan actor, 64.

Beeston, William the first, patron of Nash, 63, 64; second, his theatrical career, 65, 66; his gossip about Shakespeare, 65; his conversation, 66; Aubrey's account of, 67.

Beethoven, statue of, 233.

Beljame, M. Alexandre, on English literature, 201; death of, 201.

Benson, Mr. F. R., his company of actors, 111; his principles, 112 *seq.*; list of Shakespearean plays produced by, 114, 115 *n.*; his production of *Hamlet* unabridged, 116–18; his training of actors, 119; his services to Shakespeare, 121; his pupils on the London stage, 130.

Berkenhout, John, 195.

Betterton, Thomas, at Stratford-on-Avon, 73; contributes to Rowe's biography, 73, 76; his rendering of *Hamlet*, 101, 102.

Biography, art of, in England, 51 *seq.*

Bishop, Sir William, 76.

Bishopsgate (London), Shakespeare at, 226, 227.

Blackfriars, Shakespeare's house at, 227.

Boileau and English literature, 200.

Bolingbroke (in *Richard II.*), patriotism of, 173, 174.